THE
ROOKIE'S
PLAYBOOK

A New Teacher's Practical Playbook for
Thriving in the First Years of Teaching

Andrea "Fitz" Fitzgerald

The Rookie's Playbook

www.mentalfitzness.com
Instagram: @mentalfitzness
Facebook: @mentalfitzness

ISBN-13: 978-0-578-68705-6

Editor: Lauren Michelle
Interior Design: Lauren Michelle
Cover Design: Oladimeji Alaka

To my favorite human being, Christina, you inspire
me each day to be the best version of myself
and share that gift with others.

PART I

WELCOME TO THE TEACHING GAME

INTRODUCTION: THE MELTDOWN

I HAD A MELTDOWN—the kind you have as a kid where there's ugly crying involved. Can you relate? If so, then please follow me down the school halls with a student. At the time, I had to call this student's parents because she was disrespectful to her fellow classmates and me. New teachers, if you have not experienced a challenge like getting a student's disrespect, then lucky you! I can laugh now when I look back on how I handled this incident, but at the time, it was anything but funny.

So, here I am, believing I am speaking to the child's parents on the phone in the hallway and feeling like I had accomplished something. When I walked back into my classroom, the students were laughing hysterically. I couldn't figure out what was going on, and I couldn't get control of my class. I screamed, "BE QUIIIIIEEETTT!" They still kept laughing. I thought, *What just happened here?*

Ring! The students headed to their next class, and one student stayed behind and said, "Ms. Fitzgerald, you know you didn't talk to her parents, right?" Pausing for a second, I responded, "Yes, we did talk." Then, like an old movie reel, the entire classroom hour replayed in my mind. She proceeded to tell me that the call was made to the inside of the classroom and that everything was heard on speakerphone.

Basically, I got played by fifteen-year-olds in my first year. Yes, I called a student inside of my own classroom and *thought* I was having a conversation with a parent. The idea that my students tricked me wore me out, especially since I'd already felt the lack of respect from this challenging student. The last thing I wanted was to lose my entire classroom's respect.

I slumped into my brand-new teacher's chair at my desk and had a complete meltdown. I bashed my skills and thought that I had failed my biggest challenge. I mainly thought about the big picture, like how my lack of respect and influence could affect test scores, and how this whole "teacher's experience" was completely out of my league. How was I going to deal with the students the next day?

This was my life for most of my first year. I was leaving my class stressed or without a voice because I had zero classroom management. I screamed a lot of days, and I just couldn't get a grasp on everything that teaching required. I found myself pissed off. I knew my content. I knew how to write a lesson plan. I had the makings of a good teacher, yet here I was, stressed to the max daily.

It reminded me of my first year as a college athlete when I played pick-up basketball in the gym with my new teammates. I was dribbling the ball toward the net and I got hit on this screen so hard that it felt like I'd hit a brick wall. I fell and was in complete shock. *Welcome to college!* It was a hard transition. High school basketball was nothing like this. My first year of teaching felt very similar.... No matter how hard I tried, I couldn't seem to shake the perpetual state of shock.

I can't believe I made it through that first year. Not to say that it's challenging for everyone—I have seen some people transition nicely into their first year. However, that was not my experience. I felt so ill-prepared for actual teaching even though supposedly I had been adequately prepared.

If you can make it through years one and two, you got this. A lot of tips and best practices in teaching aren't always in the manual. Despite my epic meltdown, I actually made it in the profession. Our math team had some of the best results in the school district, and, because of our success, I was promoted to math coach and advisor. I don't say this to brag, but to tell you that I started off on pretty challenging grounds, yet here I am today, writing a book to help others make that transition go more smoothly.

One of the things I really value is practicality and tools to do what needs to get done. Have you ever received critical feedback from someone regarding your job performance, but they didn't bother to share any solutions or strategies to help you improve? Annoying, right? After several rounds of trial and error, great mentoring, and a deep desire to learn, I eventually got the hang of teaching. I became one of the top teachers in my school and produced some of the top growth measures across our district. I want to share some of the tools and strategies that have worked for me.

Before we dive into the game, I want to explain how this book is structured. It is both a book and a workbook. There are 40+ tips and strategies that will help you succeed in your first few years of teaching. After each tip, I provide an activity or action step to help you implement the strategy, and then I give you time to reflect on whether the method works for you. Feel free to add, subtract, and modify whatever you'd like.

Because I am a former athlete and an ESPN junkie, I use a lot of sports analogies in this guide. Here is the first one: you are a rookie! A rookie is defined as "*a member of an athletic team in his or her first full season in that sport.*" This is your first full season. Let's get ready for opening day!

PART II

TEACHING IS A FOUR-QUARTER GAME

TEACHING IS A FOUR-QUARTER GAME

SIMILAR TO BASKETBALL and football, the teaching game requires different versions of yourself during each quarter of the year. As an athlete, each component of the game required something different from me, my teammates, coaches, and even the referees. For pre-game, I had to mentally prepare for tip-off. In the first quarter, as a team, the goal was to start off strong and maintain that dominance throughout the first half. At halftime, our coach would give us a speech, look at the halftime stats, and make necessary adjustments. In the second half of the game, we would turn up the intensity because the stakes were higher and we wanted to win. Similarly, there are several phases throughout the school year that require different components, aspects, and adjustments within YOU!

"BE TRUE TO THE GAME, BECAUSE THE GAME WILL BE TRUE TO YOU. IF YOU TRY TO SHORTCUT THE GAME, THEN THE GAME WILL SHORTCUT YOU. IF YOU PUT FORTH THE EFFORT, GOOD THINGS WILL BE BESTOWED UPON YOU. THAT'S TRULY ABOUT THE GAME, AND IN SOME WAYS THAT'S ABOUT LIFE TOO."

—MICHAEL JORDAN

PRE-GAME: GET YOUR MIND READY FOR THE GAME

WHEN I PLAYED college basketball or any sport, one of the essential components of game day was the preparation. My pre-game routine would start well before tip-off. I would wake up early in the morning and have a healthy breakfast, preferably some type of carbs to give me energy throughout the day. Then I would go to our walkthrough, which reviewed our defensive and offensive schemes. Similarly, preparation prior to the first day of school sets you up for the entire school year. So, if there's one part of the year that you want to nail, it's this one. I did not really think about many of these components prior to teaching, so hopefully you will be more prepared than I was during my first year. In this section, we will focus on getting you and your mind game day ready. Having a strong game plan will also be important. You'll want to be prepared for tip-off so it sets you up for success for the remainder of the year.

FIRST QUARTER: FOUNDATION

Credibility. Confidence. Connection. These three attributes are going to be essential to building a strong foundation as a teacher. According to Harry Wong's book, *The First Days of School*, there was a study that found that the first three weeks of school determine the success of your class throughout the year. Same goes for a house: the foundation is critical to a house being steady and strong. Without it, the house would fall apart. Having laser-like focus in the first quarter is what sets the tone and creates a strong foundation.

In order to build the foundation, you must consistently follow through with the high, positive expectations on day one. This part of the year can be challenging because you really need to stick to your guns and be disciplined and clear on what you expect from your students. The best quote I can give you for the first quarter is: "It's easier to lighten up later in the year, versus tighten up!" If you are tight on the front end with your procedures, routines, and expectations, then you can be less firm later on. I learned this the hard way, so trust me when I say be firm. Here is a prime example: hall passes about drove me crazy. At first, I just allowed the students to go somewhere every time they asked, and after a while, it had gotten out of control. In later years, I created a procedure and set an expectation that students handle their important things in between classes. However, I would provide two emergencies per semester. Students held true to that, and, more often than not, they would go during their five-minute window between classes because I was firm and consistent. None of these strategies, tools, and tips will create a strong foundation without CONSISTENCY!

SECOND QUARTER: MAKING ADJUSTMENTS AND FINISHING THE SEMESTER STRONG

It's the second quarter of the game! How did the first quarter go? You've had some experience under your belt, and now you want to think about starting and finishing this quarter strong. In basketball, we often want to maintain or increase our lead, or, if we are behind, we want to cut it down to a manageable deficit where we could still be in the game in the second half. This is similar to teaching; you want to set yourself up for success in semester two. You don't have to be perfect, but you want your classroom and structure to be manageable enough to bounce back if necessary. I have seen classes that are so out of control that it's challenging for the teacher to reel the classroom back into shape. However, I want to tell you that it's always possible to get it back on track. If you are doing a great job and things are going well, you will want to maintain that structure but also think about how you can bolster and strengthen your classroom. I would suggest working with a coach or mentor during this quarter to support you in growing as a professional. Teaching is not a one-man sport; it requires a team to be successful. Another essential component of a sports game is how you will close the quarter, so you will also want to be thinking about how you will finish the semester strong. This will create a stronger foundation for semester two.

THIRD QUARTER: RESET

In my sophomore year, I was in a major slump. (A slump is when you aren't making shots, or you are playing poorly over a consistent amount of time.) I played so poorly that my coach demoted me from a starter to a bench warmer. This particular game, I came off the bench and, *clunk*, I missed a shot again. I thought to myself, *Here we go again! I can't buy a bucket!* I went into halftime with my head down because I was struggling, and we were down ten points. Our coach gave us a speech and reviewed the stats to make necessary adjustments. After halftime, I entered the game, scored twenty-one points, AND WE WON! What am I saying here, and what does it have to do with you as a teacher?

You will have halftime as well. Your halftime will most likely be your winter break. Just like in the game where I played poorly, we were able to step back, review the stats/data, and adjust. We even won the game! You can do the same. As a teacher, halftime is a great time to reset and get things back on track and headed in the right direction. It's an opportunity to reassess what has been working and what has not. During the hustle and bustle of day-to-day operations, this can be somewhat challenging to do. Honestly, as a new teacher, I was just trying to survive. But during halftime or school breaks, I'd get an opportunity to reflect and really identify what was working, what wasn't, and adjust accordingly. Here are some quick tips on how to **R.E.S.E.T.** your classroom:

- **Review policies, expectations, and procedures:** It's a good idea to revisit how students operate in your classroom. Use this as an opportunity to remind students what your expectations are.
- **Evaluate semester one:** I would recommend taking some time to reflect on the first semester so you can identify what worked and pinpoint areas to improve your classroom.
- **Set new expectations:** After you evaluate semester one and determine the areas you want to change in your classroom, you'll want to communicate and share those new expectations with your students.
- **Establish yourself...again:** You almost want to act like this is the first day of school, and you want to prepare similarly for your first day back from a break.
- **Tone builds trust:** Tone cannot be built without consistency. You will need to be consistent and follow through with your new expectations or they will not work.

FOURTH QUARTER: GREAT PLAYERS ARE MADE IN THE OFF-SEASON

Well, you made it! As I told you earlier, if you can make it through the first year or two, the rest will fall into place. I promise you it gets easier. As you are ending your season, this is a great opportunity for you to reflect and get honest about your first-year experience.

The "off-season" (aka the summer) is a great time to work on areas that you may need to improve for next year. Every year in my classroom, I learned what was effective and ineffective and made adjustments based on the previous year. For example, I struggled with losing a lot of calculators in my class and not having assigned seats. The following year, when I was preparing my classroom, I numbered my desks and my calculators. This way, each one of my students would have an assignment for both. It made my classroom so much easier to manage. Again, I would challenge you to find a mentor or coach to gather feedback on how you could improve. We often have blind spots that we are unaware of, and a mentor or coach moves you there faster. (Check out game tip #42 later in the book to get more clarity on how you can level yourself up in the off-season.)

Major Key Alert: This summer, I encourage you to rest. Teaching can be emotionally, spiritually, and physically draining, so please use the summer to take care of yourself and replenish. We all need self-care in our lives. Relax. Release. Reset. One summer, I would work out in the morning, go hang with friends, and come home in the evening and do absolutely nothing. I mean it—nothing. Please turn it off for a bit and get some of that good summertime self-care!

"UNFORTUNATELY, THERE SEEMS TO BE FAR MORE OPPORTUNITY OUT THERE THAN ABILITY.... WE SHOULD REMEMBER THAT GOOD FORTUNE OFTEN HAPPENS WHEN OPPORTUNITY MEETS WITH PREPARATION."

—THOMAS A. EDISON

PART III

PRE-GAME

PRE-GAME TIP #1: SHARE YOUR STORY

"The most influential teacher I had was Mr. Loyd. He drank soy milk and read us Shakespeare at the beginning of every class. He also allowed us to read whatever we wanted silently the last five minutes of class."

—Robert Johnson, ninth grade

EXPANSION. CREATIVITY. ACCEPTANCE.

CONNECTION IS THE opportunity for us to get to know ourselves and others. We all have a unique story to tell. What makes these stories so significant to others is that it allows one to not only see that we are human, but that we are relatable and equally significant in our experiences. So, what story do you believe will impact a student and allow him or her to really get to know you? What story will allow them to remember you and also affect them in their life experiences five, ten, or twenty years from now?

Even though our students are different in age, we are humans at our core. Many years ago, I had a student teacher who was brilliant. He scored a thirty-six on the ACT, but the students didn't care about his content knowledge. I would run to the copy machine, and by the time I got back, the class would be completely out of control because this teacher lacked necessary people skills. Connection comes before curriculum. Sharing your story builds credibility, connection, and evokes emotion. It establishes a strong foundation from the onset of the year, which makes teaching your actual content a lot easier. People "do" people. One of the things you want to think about is what lessons or experiences you have had in your life thus far that you want to share. My favorite teachers were the ones that were REAL. They had a unique story and brought their authentic selves to the class. One of the teachers that comes to mind is Ms. Wildman, my African American Literature teacher. I'm not going to lie, when she greeted me at the door, I was shocked. I thought, *How is this lady with blonde hair and blue eyes going to teach me about African American Literature?* She walked to the front of the class and told our class that she was Pentecostal, she would wear skirts each day, and she would bring her full self to our class.

Honestly, she did not have to share that information. She simply could have taught the class, but she created an experience by being her authentic self and sharing her story. I don't remember the content, but I remember her.

As new teachers, "who we be" and our stories help set the stage for the experience we create for our students. We are teachers, yes, but stories are what connect us all. On day one, you want to think of yourself as a speaker who's sharing a powerful message to your audience. Everybody has unique life experiences that they can use to connect and build credibility with students.

There was a teacher that I supported in preparing for the first day of school—we spent the majority of our time crafting his opening day speech. Initially, we started with him sharing his unique life experiences and timeline. He stated he had a variety of jobs: he was a fireman, a teacher, a bodybuilder, and several other things. As we continued to collaborate, the big idea of his teaching style was "variety." His story was: *I know what it's like to struggle getting up, and I'm going to help you get there through math.*

Another essential piece you want to share on day one is your "why" for teaching. Students want to understand why they should even listen to you. They want to know that you have a genuine interest in their success.

A few things to consider in terms of your story:

- What are the three most impactful moments in your life thus far? Why?
- What are the big life lessons that you've experienced thus far?
- What's your "why" for teaching?
- How did you grow up? Are parts of it relatable to your audience?
- What was school like for you growing up?
- What roles and jobs have you had that have led you to this point?

Here is a sample of my opening day speech:

My name is Ms. Fitzgerald, and I'm going to be your Algebra I teacher for this school year. I'm super excited about the opportunity to teach you guys. My story is that I am a former athlete, so my teaching style is a bit like a coach's in the sense that I am going to push you to your limits because I know your greatness. I've worked in the NBA for several years, and I've sat in the same seats that you guys have sat in. This is more than a job to me. I want to empower you to create an opportunity for whatever it is that you want to accomplish, whether that be college, trade school, or entrepreneurship.

Now write your sample opening day speech:

My name is _____. I'm excited to be your _____ teacher this school year. My "why" for teaching is_____

_____.

Three things I want you to know about me are:

_____, _____, and _____.

Close it strong! What is the principle or idea that you want them to keep in mind this year? (E.g., work hard, maximum effort, etc.)

Practice: Practice your opening speech with your friends and family and get feedback on how you can strengthen your message.

Visit mentalfitzness.com/resources to review my sample opening speech.

Prime Time Player: To push yourself, post a part of your intro on Instagram and tag @mentalfitzness and hashtag #openingdayspeech.

PRE-GAME TIP #2: WHAT'S YOUR "RUN OF SHOW"?

I remember each Sunday I would be sitting on my couch dreading going back to school the next day because my classroom was so chaotic. I would think to myself, *Today will be another day of me getting run over and screaming.* I was bringing home gobs and gobs of paper, leaving class each day hoarse or with no voice, and my students probably didn't learn anything because of my lack of classroom management. I thought the teaching and content knowledge would be enough, but I completely forgot about the humans that I would be interacting with. I also had to teach them how to interact and engage in the classroom. As a new teacher, you may not have thought about those things yet. That's okay, so RELAX!

As discussed in the previous section, when we thought about who we are, how do you want certain aspects of yourself to come to life in your classroom? For example, because I love sports, I broke my class into quarters:

First Quarter	Students enter the classroom and complete 2–3 math problems
Second Quarter	Instructional activities (concept development, explaining, questioning, modeling, guided practice, collaborative groups, discussions)
Third Quarter	Individual practice, partner work/practice
Fourth Quarter	Closing: ending activity/problem to check if your students got it

This may not work for you, but I want you to consider who you are and how you can create an experience that works for you and your students. For example, I knew I wasn't that organized, so students had to text their answers with a technology system into my computer because I did not like paperwork; it would always accumulate on my desk. My students really liked this setup because they loved using their phones, so being able to use technology created more student interest in the lessons.

I want you to consider your "run of show." In event management, a "run of show" is an item by item sequence of events that will happen within a show. Consider that each day in your class is a "show." It's simply a detailed outline of your class with time stamps. You want to think about what are the most essential things to do and how do you want your students to interact during each phase of the class?

Time Stamp	Activity	Notes
Pre-game (prior to bell ringing)—2 minutes into class	Gather instructional materials (sharpen pencils, grab calculator, notebooks)	Take attendance during this time, attendance slips, etc. Print **Do Now** prior to class (**Do Now** is the activity you want students to complete as they enter your class, hence the title of "**Do Now**")

Bell rings— 5 minutes	Complete **Do Now** and complete pre-game activities	**Do Now** placed on table located by the door
2–3 minutes	Recap **Do Now**	Review **Most Highly Missed Question** and determine what students need help with based on comments
1–2 minutes	Lesson intro— connect to prior knowledge	
30 minutes	Lesson activities (meat of the lesson, modeling, practice, student engagement activities)	Meat of the lesson, instructional decisions based on the heart of the standard

3–5 minutes	Synthesis, summary of the lesson— closure of the lesson	
5 minutes	Exit ticket and cool down	Assess mastery of today's lesson and what adjustments can be made for tomorrow's lesson. Also, consider what you want students to walk away with from today's lesson.

Keep in mind that the run of the show is simply a framework to provide the structures and conditions to move through the lesson. I've been in several classrooms where the content doesn't come to life for kids until the structures are there to make it happen.

Just like you teach them your specific content, you will have to teach them how to engage in your run of show as well, but you can't do that without having a framework for them to follow or thinking ahead about what you actually want in class.

Practice: Create a "run of show" for your class.

PRE-GAME TIP #3: ARRANGE YOUR CLASSROOM

Classroom setup is a key component of great teaching and learning. Oftentimes, it helps with the implementation of your "run of show" and strong classroom management. I didn't quite understand the importance of that until I started teaching. For example, you want to think about the most efficient and productive way in which the components of your "run of show" come to life. Also, think about who you are and what works for you. I wanted all the pre-game (sharpening pencils, gathering calculators, etc.) to be taken care of prior to or within the first few minutes of class, so I created a path for them upon entering the room in which they could gather these items as they entered. I placed a table by the doorway for bell work/entry activity/Do Now so that it was the first item they grabbed when they came into class. After they picked up their activity, I knew that my students would pass the chalkboard, so

I placed my calculators in a shoe rack strategically by the board.

In terms of arranging your classroom, talk to your administrator to see if you can visit your classroom prior to the administration week or during the summer at some point. The longer you have to work with your room, the better. Oftentimes, teachers have 1–2 weeks to prepare their classrooms in addition to all of the administrative preparations for day one. Visiting your classroom will allow you to see what resources are available to you, determine additional requests from the building engineer, or what you may have to purchase to create an inviting and positive experience for your students.

You also want to consider the arrangement of your desk and the students' desks. Ask yourself: Do you want them to work in groups or as individuals? If in groups, how many in each group? When I first started teaching, I couldn't manage my class well, so I had an individual setup for my students because I wanted to learn their names. I was afraid to allow them to work in groups because my classroom management was not very strong, and I did not want to lose control of my class. However, now I understand the importance of having students in *groups to collaborate.* According to Cornell

University, strong student collaboration contributes to "*development of higher-level thinking, oral communication, self-management, and leadership skills. Promotion of student-faculty interaction. Increase in student retention, self-esteem, and responsibility.*" One of the essential pieces you want to keep in mind is you will have to create structures around collaborative groups.

Rookie questions to consider:

- What type of experience do I want to create for students?
- How many tables/desks do I have?
- How do I want to arrange them? In pairs? Triads? Quads? Individual rows?
- Where do I want to position my entry activity?
- Are there any adjustments to my run of show?

Practice: Reach out to an administrator and take a field trip to your classroom and complete inventory for your classroom.

What's in your class?

Classroom Inventory	Number of Items	How do you want to arrange it?
1. Desks		
2. Teacher Desks		
3.		
4.		
5.		

What do you need to add or purchase for your classroom? Once you've determined that, draw a mock-up of how you want to arrange all of the available resources in your class.

"STRUCTURE SIGNIFICANTLY INFLUENCES BEHAVIOR, THEREBY DRAMATICALLY IMPACTING RESULTS."

—CHRIS HUTCHINSON

PRE-GAME TIP #4: CREATE A SYSTEM TO SUPPORT THE SETUP AND ARRANGEMENT

SYSTEMS. SYSTEMS. SYSTEMS. Having no systems almost took me out in my first year. I had no idea that it was imperative to have systems in place. My first year, my co-teacher and I had a seventh-period class that was "off the chain." That class was wild, and we always said that we had no business teaching anybody's kid that year because it was so chaotic. I would yell at the top of my lungs daily. I would try to enforce things, and they would not even listen to me. I was working really hard, but I hadn't figured out how to transfer that to my most valuable resource: my students.

When having no system goes bad: Each class was assigned 35 calculators, and by the end of the year, do you know how many I had? Maybe 10–12. I lost

23 calculators at $100 apiece—that's $2,300, and I probably lost more. Why? Because I had no system for how the calculators would be organized or how students would pick them up and place them back. I decided that I would create a system where my desks were numbered, and each student would have a calculator assigned to that number, and I would have a shoe rack placed in the front of the classroom with calculator numbers. That way, I wouldn't lose them. During the last minute of class, I would ask all the students to return the calculators. Therefore, I would know which calculator was missing and which student to talk to about it.

Now, return to your "run of show" and classroom map/arrangement. Where do you need a system, procedure, or routine? You may not know where you need a system—again, you are learning, and that's okay. The question you may want you to ask yourself is: How do I want them to engage with the various components of my "run of show"? What routines and procedures do I want to use? Take a second and imagine you are a student in your own class. What is the experience you want them to have?

Just like how you teach your students your specific content area, you also have to teach them your own classroom systems, routines, and procedures. Having a clear set of procedures will save you many headaches. After a while, your systems become second nature, not only for you but for your students, which allows you to focus more on teaching actual content. One teacher that I coached had a lot of knowledge to share with his students. He was a math whiz. Students would often enter his class, and he would attempt to enforce rules and teach. However, the students were unresponsive because there were no systems or procedures in place to create a space for actual teaching and learning. Needless to say, most of his time was spent redirecting behavior, as opposed to teaching math. The underlying component of this is high expectations and consistency, which we will dive into later when discussing culture. Systems are great, but we must also implement and execute them.

Here are a few suggestions to consider when thinking about where a system may be needed. I also provided a sample of what I did in my class if you need some ideas:

- **Taking attendance:** I often took attendance in the system while they were doing their entry activity.

- **Entry routine:** A few minutes to handle pre-game or before-class activities (including gathering materials, sharpening pencils, grabbing calculators), 5 minutes to complete the entry activity, enter answers in CPS technology and review data, then 2–3 minutes on the whiteboard to review the most missed question and explain the answer. After that, jump into the lesson.

- **Hall passes:** In my class, students get two passes per semester. When reviewing the syllabus, explain to your students that they have five minutes between classes, and the expectation is to handle their personal matters during that time. But also explain that you understand emergencies happen, and, therefore, each student has a set number of passes per quarter. (**Disclaimer:** This is no way to insinuate being the "bathroom police," but more about having some guidelines in place. At times, I would loosen my guidelines because I better understood my students. Understanding your audience will be critical in discerning whether or not you should give a student a hall pass out.)

- **Group collaboration and/or group work**: Assign roles and numbers to your groups, then have a finished product due at the end of the collaboration. This creates accountability for students, and they are more motivated and inclined to do the work.

- **Passing papers to the front**: Students pass their papers to the front of their rows. Once all the papers get to the front, the first student in each row passes the work to his or her right. The student sitting in the first seat of the last column gives me all the work.

- **How and when to exit the class**: Rookie, make sure you are ready to dismiss kids at the bell. Set your routines for closing down shop with ample time. Holding kids past the bell creates a host of problems, including getting kids in trouble for being late to their next class. Instead of rushing out of class, we want to ensure that all calculators or equipment are returned, our areas are cleaned up, and exit ticket.

- **Assigned seats**: Every student is assigned a seat at the beginning of the year (I will create a seating chart to maintain a pulse on correct seats and adjustments that may be needed). Having assigned seats allows students to interact with one another, and it builds community and structure in your classroom. An additional thing to consider is understanding that the classroom is dynamic and continuously evolves, so I often would continue to switch seats throughout the year so that students could interact with multiple and diverse groups.

Once you have your classroom arranged, think about the systems you want to have in place to help your class run smoothly. It takes the guess work out for you and your students, and most of all, it creates consistency, which builds trust. I'm going to give you an example of how important consistency is:

My local McDonald's milkshake machine has been broken since I was five years old. I know that if I visit that restaurant tomorrow and ask for a milkshake, they are going to say, "Our machine is broken." Conversely, if I go to Chick-fil-A and say, "Hey, I would like twenty hot sauces and five honey mustards for my five nuggets," they are going to say, "My pleasure." One thing I know about both is that they are consistent. They have created an expectation of what will happen by doing the same thing each time I visit. The same thing applies to your classroom. How consistent we are is what determines the flow and tone of our classrooms. The procedures and routines work if you are consistent. Without those structures, it can be challenging to teach any content.

Practice: Return to your "run of show" and identify what systems and procedures you want to create. Also, how will you teach systems and routines to your students? How will you evaluate if they are effective and efficient?

PRE-GAME TIP #5: ESTABLISH YOUR ENTRY ROUTINE

When it comes to managing a classroom, it is imperative that you set the tone from the start. One of the best ways to give students a glimpse of your expectations is with your entry routine. The first part of your class sets the tone for the other systems in your class and creates conditions and culture for great teaching and learning. As a coach, I have seen both the good and the bad, and I can assure you that in classes where there was not a strong, consistent entry routine, oftentimes, the classroom management and structure was off, which really affected student achievement.

This is the component of your class that you want to master, and it starts on day one. Even though most teachers don't necessarily teach content on the first day—instead, they often choose to focus more on rules and policies—you'll want to model the experience and expectation around entering Mr. or Ms. _____'s class. It also allows you to handle attendance, tardies, and additional administrative duties while students are engaged in their entry activity.

- Do you want to greet them at the door?
- Do you want to give a handout to students each day?
- Do you want your bell work to be on the board?
- Where will they get the materials needed for the class?
- How long will they have for each part of the entry routine?

But how do I do this? How? Glad you asked. Simply start with what you would like the first five minutes of your class to look, sound, and feel like. Answer the prompt below.

What would you like the first five minutes of your class to look, sound, and feel like?

Here is an example of the system I created for my entry routine:

I want students to enter the class. As they enter, I would like to give them a high five and hand them their entry assignment. After that, I would like for them to complete all of their pre-game activities (sharpen pencil, grab calculator, technology, etc.), but taking no longer than two minutes after the bell rings. I would like for them to silently complete the entry activity within five minutes, which is how much time they will be given before the timer goes off. Students will pass up their Do Now with thirty seconds on the clock so that the hand-in process is completed quickly and efficiently. I will then set my timer for three minutes and briefly review the most commonly missed problem and answer one question from one student in the entire class. Once that's done, I will review the data to determine which concepts I may need to review in tomorrow's Do Now activity.

Students became so familiar with this routine that if I forgot to have an entry assignment ready, or even if I wrote it on the board instead of passing it out as they walked in, they would be asking, "Where is our daily quiz?" As noted in the previous tip, consistency is the key to effective implementation, and you want to rehearse and practice it over and over so that students are familiar with how to enter your class.

Practice: Establish your entry routine and create a plan on how to teach/practice with students the first few days of school.

"ONE THING THAT MAKES IT POSSIBLE TO BE AN OPTIMIST IS IF YOU HAVE A CONTINGENCY PLAN FOR WHEN ALL HELL BREAKS LOOSE."

—RANDY PAUSCH

PRE-GAME TIP #6: CREATE A CONTINGENCY PLAN

OKAY, LET'S PRETEND you have prepared for a trip to Jamaica. You have your bags packed, you have your new vacation outfits ready, and you are excited to hop on the plane and get to your destination. You arrive at the airport, and your flight is delayed. The attendant tells you that because of the significant delay, you will miss your connecting flight. The flight attendant starts looking at other flights to get you to your destination as quickly as possible. You will arrive in Jamaica, but you will be taking a different route. I imagine most of us have experienced having a well-laid plan and itinerary, yet something happens, and we have to adjust. The airline was prepared for possible delays, cancellations, etc., as they have several flights going in and out of the airport each day. Therefore, often they are prepared because they know things happen regardless of how great the plan is prepared. What they have is a contingency plan, which is going to be another key component in your classroom.

My first couple of years, I would be going hard in the paint on Sunday night—I mean hard, y'all! I was staying up until 12:00 a.m. creating my lesson plans, but what I wasn't prepared for was how to work with teenagers or reroute when the plan went to shit.

At this point, we have created our run of show, classroom setup, and systems, but what happens when they fall flat? What happens when there is a delay? What if a student is late? What if a student doesn't have paper?

What if? What if? What if? The list could go on and on, but you want to think about what happens when some of these things don't happen, or when a boundary is crossed with you in terms of your setup and flow of class.

Believe it or not, pencils helped me learn more about a contingency plan. As a math teacher, it was a requirement to write in pencil, but for whatever reason, I often found that students did not have them. At first, I would complain about the students not being prepared to work—"these kids aren't ever ready." However, I realized "these kids" wanted and needed to learn, regardless if they had a pencil or not.

I would later learn that sometimes they did not even have access to one. With that in mind, I came up with a contingency plan. I decided to use my teacher supply money and buy lots of boxes of pencils. If they asked for a pencil, they could have one in exchange for collateral, whether it be a shoe, a phone charger, a notebook, something to ensure that I would get that pencil back. Another strategy I have seen other teachers use is passing out pencils or pens at the beginning of class and picking them up at the end of class.

The contingency plan is about thinking ahead and preparing for the delay in your flight or lesson plan. By having a plan in place in advance, you build trust with your students by being well prepared and providing a structured environment. Additionally, it eliminates some of the stress when shit hits the fan. My coach often says that you want to work on your snapback resilience—meaning, in life, shit's going to hit the fan, but it's okay. It's all about snapping back and getting on track. Your snapback game will be much easier if you have a plan B in place, as you'll want to be able to spend your time on teaching actual content, not managing students.

Practice: Return to your run of show and think about all of the potential "delays" or mishaps that could possibly hinder your implementation of the plan. Identify a contingency for each one.

Here are just a few to get you started:

If this happens...	Then I will...
No pencil	Have students provide collateral in exchange for a pencil.
Tardy for class	Have a tardy log by the door to track tardies. Call parents after two tardies.
Absent	Students will have three days to make up any missed assignments.
No paper	I will provide paper for all students regardless of why they don't have it.

"CULTURE IS THE HEARTBEAT OF YOUR CLASSROOM. HOW WILL YOUR HEART PUMP THIS YEAR?"

—ANDREA FITZGERALD

PRE-GAME TIP #7: BUILDING CULTURE AND RELATIONSHIPS

Me: "Everette is going really hard at math this year.
What changed?"
Everette's mom: "He likes his teacher!"

WHEN I ENTERED the classroom, I had the makings of a good teacher. I knew how to write a lesson plan, I knew math content, but I did not know the importance of these two things: building culture and relationships. Honestly, this is what ticked me off after I was teaching for a while. No one told me that, in the words of Rita Pearson, "Kids don't learn from people they don't like." Jayson Gaddis, a world-renowned relationship expert, coined the phrase "both connection and curriculum." Man, I wish I knew that. I would sum that up by saying that not just kids, but people in general, don't go hard for people they don't like. My struggle for the first couple of years was grounded in not building solid relationships and having a strong culture in my classroom. I had received some bad advice as I started out that you had to be mean to the kids and "not smile" for them to respect you. That did not work, and I was totally being inauthentic. I'm not the "no smile" type; I am a dorky jock. I had to find my way and bring my full authentic self to the table.

Think about your heart; it's the most powerful organ in our body. Once it stops beating, unfortunately, that's it! It's only the size of a fist, but it ensures that the blood flows properly throughout our bodies and supports all of our other systems. Culture and relationships are the heartbeats of our classrooms. If it's off, our classrooms will be in heart failure. If you have ever seen the show *Sanford and Son*, one of the main characters would often say, "It's the big one, Elizabeth!" whenever he felt like he was having heart trouble. My classroom was in heart failure for many days because of this missing piece.

It didn't matter how much knowledge I had if I couldn't connect and engage with the most valuable resource: students. As I mentioned earlier in the book, as a coach, I have observed over 400 classrooms, and often it's not the most knowledgeable teacher that gets the best results. It's the teachers with strong connections, content knowledge, and pedagogy.

I want to ensure that your classroom has the best heart health possible. Below I listed five principles that will significantly impact the "heart health" of your classroom. This is simply what has worked in my classroom. Feel free to add or subtract and find what works for you. I will utilize a section for each one of the following concepts to take us deeper and give you a better understanding. Remember, 80 percent of teaching is all about relationships and understanding that the teacher and student are complex human beings.

- Set positive, high expectations
- Examine your own bias (what's getting in the way of the connection?)
- Be authentic—real recognizes real
- Relate to, know, and connect with your audience
- Be trustworthy and consistent

I want you to think about the best job you've ever had and explain why you enjoyed working there.

My favorite job was:

I enjoyed working there because:

My worst job was:

I didn't care to work there because:

These are two unique experiences, and I'm sure vastly different experiences with each organization. Why? Because culture is the "mindset" or thinking of an organization, and that determines how a company moves and acts. This applies to our classrooms as well—culture is the "mindset" of our classroom, and it impacts the effectiveness of how we implement the content.

No Culture = No Learning

Practice: Imagine the type of culture you would like to have in your classroom. Write a vision of your classroom culture.

PRE-GAME TIP #8: SET POSITIVE, HIGH EXPECTATIONS

"In classrooms where teachers held higher expectations, students gained more than four months."

—The Opportunity Myth

Kids will rise to the bar that we set. Let me say that again: kids will rise to the bar that we set. I've heard educators say, "These kids don't know how to act." I think it's the complete opposite. The X factor in a classroom is you and me. Charles Barkley said it best: "It's not about X's and O's, it's all about the Jimmys and the Joes," meaning the best laid plans happen with solid players. And you, my friend, are a solid player/teacher in the making. My first few years, this was quite confusing to me: How was it that some students would be all over the place in my class, but completely well-mannered and behaving in another teacher's class?

For example, my co-teacher Ms. Malone and I were on the struggle bus and could not figure out how to get a grasp on management in our seventh-period class. Our motto for that class is "Never Forget," because even though both of us are successful in the educational field now, that first year almost took us out and helped us become successful educators. One of the veteran teachers sat us down and told us about the teacher next door, Ms. Dickenson. He recommended that we observe her in action and watch how she managed and set the bar in her class. I remember him saying, "XYZ student may act up in other classes, but in her math class, he knows what the expectations are, so he operates on a completely different level." Bottom line: it starts with us and our expectations.

There was a study conducted by The New Teacher Project (TNTP) called *The Opportunity Myth*, where they researched a variety of students' schooling experiences. The study found that four key things benefit ALL students: high expectations, instructional materials, engagement, and instruction. What do you think was the highest indicator in terms of achievement? You guessed it—high expectations. Expectations shape so much in our classrooms, and setting those standards determines how we manage our class and the work we put in front of our students.

I will own that my expectations were somewhat low when I first became a teacher, and my end-of-year data mirrored that. My first year, only 25 percent of my students scored proficient. I would often focus only on the students who I felt could do the work.

As I began improving my expectations, it changed my perceptions. Once I believed that ALL students could do the work, it altered what I believed was possible in my class. I would not stop until they "got it," and I would continue to push them. It's also important to support your students to help them get there. Yes, I was relentless, but I also supported them with tools, strategies, and additional help. I would stay after school, I would offer my planning period—heck, I'd even come to school on Saturday in order to help them achieve mastery. When we believe in something, we find unique ways to achieve success despite what may seem like insurmountable odds.

In Stephen Covey's book, *The Seven Habits of Highly Effective People*, Covey shares a story about two different classrooms and how positive and high expectations had an impact on the students. The two classrooms were separated based on their previous year's performance level. The administration grouped the "high-flyers" in one class and placed the "low-performing" students in the other class. The administration mixed up the records and told the teachers that the "high-flyers" were the "low-performing" students and vice versa. At the end of the year, who do you think scored the highest?

You guessed it—the class with the "low-performing" students. The administration was shocked by the data and asked the teacher how they did it. The teacher responded, "I knew how smart and capable they were, so when one way didn't work, I found another way to help them learn." Say it one more time for the people in the back: a large portion of great teaching is based on your positive, high expectations.

Our students have high ambitions, and it is our duty, obligation, and responsibility to believe in them and set the bar high. If we don't believe in them, our students will sense that and disengage. Students are extremely aware, and I promise you they will rise to the bar if you push them there.

My last year, when I left the classroom, I wanted to write my students a letter. I wrote one...threw it away. Wrote another...threw it away. Finally, I told myself, *I'm going to write from my heart.* And when I finally finished, I realized this is why I teach. I teared up as I told them, "I know your secret." They were all giving me confused looks. The secret was, "I know your brilliance. I know what you're capable of. I know how amazing you are. Because I know your brilliance, I'm relentless in what I expect. No, I will not let you put your head down. Yes, I will create structures and an environment to support great teaching and learning. Yes, I will challenge you to show me your brilliance while still supporting you along the way. No, I will not lower the bar because I know you can meet it."

Practice: What are the expectations you want to have in your classroom?

PRE-GAME TIP #9: EXAMINE YOUR OWN BIAS

When I was in school, our teachers did not allow us to use calculators, so when I first became a math teacher, it was odd that some of my students were so reliant on calculators for basic math. I came up with the notion that because they needed to use their calculators, they were unable to do math. At one point, I even refused to allow my students to use their calculators so they could learn math the "right way"—meaning the way I learned. I was about to pull my hair out because not very much math was taking place. One day, I was sharing my concerns with the district advisor, and she asked me, "Are you teaching algebra or arithmetic?" I replied, "Algebra." She then told me, "If the calculator is a helpful tool to support them with access to do algebra, let them use it. The end of year exam will not test your ninth-grade math class on third-grade arithmetic." That was a super reflective moment for me because I connected the dots and understood that students were not learning because of my own ego and bias. I was judging my students and had boxed them in, as well as their abilities, based on my own experiences. I thought that they couldn't do it, when, in fact, the calculator was a mathematical tool to support them in class.

When I allowed my students to utilize the calculators as a tool, their scores went through the roof. They were capable of so much more than I was giving them credit for. My own bias had created an inequitable environment for my students. Aperture Education states that implicit bias reduces the opportunity for educational equity in our classrooms. But what is educational equity? According to Equity Advocate Tamera Malone, "Equity is every kid getting their academic, social, and emotional needs met so they can reach their full potential." Equity in education is not about treating students the exact same, but treating students fairly regardless of socioeconomic status, gender, race, or other circumstances. This starts with owning our own biases. Being honest with and examining ourselves is some of the most challenging work that we will ever do. Who wants to admit that they have a bias? I still have biases, and I've been in the game for a while. The key is to be willing to dig deeper and uncover those biases and change them. When you discover your bias, it's okay. There's nothing wrong with you. We are human, and we all have unique experiences that will impact how we show up in the world and view certain situations.

According to the National Association for Multicultural Education, "*We may try to be neutral, but we all have values, beliefs, and predispositions that impact how we relate to others.*" The key is to get real and honest about them. By being self-aware, we have a better chance of changing our thinking. It is my belief that awareness is one of the most powerful tools in the universe, because, in the words of Iyanla Vanzant, "*We cannot repair what we are not aware of.*" My own bias was based on students using a calculator. Ouch! Hard to accept, but so true. I treated my students differently based on that bias and did not believe that they could do the work. And my students' scores were a reflection of that belief.

As teachers, this essential piece of self-reflection and self-examination is often missed as we get caught up in the hustle and bustle of everyday life. Be aware of these things so they don't get in the way of you or your students being successful. *"The fundamental fight or flight response is actually an example of unconscious bias. It is based on what feels safe to us in a certain situation. Our experiences, our preferences, our education, our upbringing all contribute to the model of the world we have, and it makes us who we are. That is not necessarily a bad thing—it becomes problematic when we start treating groups of people as less favorable, or we make bad decisions based on that model."*

—Candice Bosteels,
Founder and Managing Director of IdentiCy

Practice: Be honest with yourself. Try and notice, without judgment, when you exhibit bias. Jot those moments down.

How do these moments of bias inform how you treat others? Yourself? How do you show up in the moment or even the next day after reflecting?

"LESS PERFECTION. MORE AUTHENTICITY."

—ANONYMOUS

PRE-GAME TIP #10: BE AUTHENTIC

AS I MENTIONED earlier, during my first year, I was told to gain respect from students by refusing to smile and cracking the proverbial whip. I tried it. I tried to be a raging b——. I tried to be a hardcore teacher. I can confirm it doesn't work. And, most importantly, it was not me. The kids knew it, too, and they really wanted to see the real Ms. Fitzgerald. You gain a lot more respect and can build more solid connections if you are your full, authentic self. If I'm honest, I had no idea who the real Ms. Fitzgerald was when I first started, but as I became more self-aware, I evolved into a much stronger teacher because I was willing to bring my full self each day. Students want to connect with us. They don't need another fake person standing up in front of them pretending like they care. I found that by being real and genuinely caring, students would go above and beyond for me.

They will do the same for you, but you must be your authentic self. Students tend to be more uncensored than adults. They do not have the same filters in place that adults do, nor do they subscribe to the norms of what they "should" do or say.

Case in point: my first year, I was ballin' on a budget (i.e., new teacher pay). I wore the same black pants every day and would switch up the shirts. Don't judge me—yes, I wore the same pants every single day. It was the only pair of dress pants that I had, and I was so thankful for Fridays because we were able to wear jeans. That way, I could make good use of my one pair of black pants.

One day, I tried to call a student out, and she told me, "You wear the same pants every day." I had no response for that; I was almost at a standstill because, dang it, she was right. That Sunday, I ran to Macy's and bought four pairs of pants. I thought, *Man, I'm totally embarrassed about getting called out, but I appreciate her honesty.* That incident taught me that kids see things that we often don't. Or, if we do see them, we're often too hesitant to say anything. To be authentic, we must be self-aware. How can we bring the real us if we aren't aware of ourselves? Always remember that our students are watching our every move.

As I became more aware of myself, I was able to bring a better version of myself to my students daily. As for the raging b— that I tried to be, I transformed into something completely different. I realized that my teaching style was more like that of a coach. I am a dorky jock, and I knew how to make typically boring things exciting, push students to their limits, but also support them while reaching their goals. As a teacher, my results were pretty impressive, considering some of the challenges we faced in an urban school. Students with a 0.3 percent chance of scoring proficient at the beginning of the year were able to be proficient despite the 99.7 percent projection data from the state saying that it was impossible. In my class, I was relentless in terms of my expectations. Despite the grim data, students were willing to go the distance. They would work hard, consistently challenging themselves and each other. Why? I was able to connect with them. To be authentic, it requires a certain layer of vulnerability. Be willing to show that you aren't this perfect adult that makes no mistakes, but you are a human being with feelings, emotions, and flaws.

Warning: Being authentic does not mean being the students' friend. Being authentic is more so about showing that you are a genuine, caring, complex human being who has your students' best interest at heart.

Bonus: Know yourself and your triggers (i.e., the things that could potentially set you off). This is really important. As we think about students and their increased levels of awareness, it's essential that we know what could potentially set us off. Once we identify those things, what should we do to mitigate potential triggers and respond differently? I've been ticked off to the point where I did and said things that I regretted. How do we foresee our triggers and make a plan in advance of how to respond?

Game Tip Reflection Journal: What are your top three superpowers? Where are your areas for growth? How could you leverage those strengths in the classroom? What adjustments need to be made? How self-aware do you think you are? Go to mentalfitzness.com/resources to complete the self-awareness reflection tool to learn how to leverage your strengths in the classroom.

PRE-GAME TIP #11: RELATE TO, KNOW, AND CONNECT WITH YOUR AUDIENCE

This is one of the most important yet neglected skills that's not taught prior to teaching.

Relationships determine how well your class will flow. Kids don't learn from people they don't like or relate to. No, you do not have to be just like your students or even from the same background, because I certainly was not. You can still build relationships with your students. When I was a student, my teacher taught, and we listened and took notes, no questions asked. I once heard that "even if you are from different worlds, if people feel seen and understood, they will go the distance for you." Not quite the experience I had when I first started teaching. Gone are the days of the teacher just standing at the whiteboard. Teaching requires so much more. If you can master building relationships with the students, then teaching pedagogy is not as challenging. I call this part the softer side of education because this piece is probably not in your teacher education program. This was one of the most challenging areas of teaching for me. I thought to myself, *I shouldn't have to do all of this just to teach*, but, in my opinion, this is the most essential part of teaching.

One of the things I had to consider was that it wasn't about me. At first, I took a lot of things that my students did personally. When they didn't bring back homework, when they made smart-ass comments, when they refused to pay attention in class—anything. Remember, it's not personal. Most times, it has nothing to do with you. My frustration came from not knowing my students or understanding who they were and their backgrounds. The hardest decision I had to make as a kid was whether to wear Reebok or Nike to hoop in, and I knew when I finished hooping that I would have a home-cooked meal on the table. As I began teaching, I discovered that it wasn't the same for all of my students. I used to get so frustrated with one of my students because he was late every single day. However, the truth was that he woke himself up every morning because his mom worked. The biggest lesson I learned from that experience was compassion. Being a teacher starts with understanding your audience.

For example, I have been training for a marathon. I had convinced my best friend to train with me even though she's more of a weightlifter. I told her that I would lead the training. So, the first day, we headed to the park, and the plan started with two miles. We started running, and I felt amazing. However, she started walking rather quickly and waved her hand to say "go ahead" without her. After we finished running, she said, "You are a terrible coach!" I was thinking, *Why, the plan said two miles*? She said, "I've never run like that, and you just threw me out in the deep end." The truth, she was right. I was a terrible coach that day because I did not consider my audience. I came back the next day with an adjusted plan. We still ran two miles, but we ran for two minutes and walked for one so that we could build her stamina.

When we don't consider or get to know our students, it is just like me with the two-mile running plan and thinking that just because the plan said two miles straight, that's what it had to be. Incorrect. I adjusted the plan after I considered my audience; however, I still maintained high expectations of getting in the two miles. She gave me the feedback, and I received it. What would have happened if she hadn't given me feedback or I was unable to receive and adjust? I didn't lower my standards, but I provided the support and stayed by her side.

As teachers, we do the same thing. We are not lowering the bar, just taking the space to truly understand who they are. Building relationships and understanding your students is analogous to love: it offers challenges *and* support. If we challenge without support, people run away. If we support too much without challenge, we enable our students. It's all about finding the perfect balance of offering both to our students.

Practice: What is your strategy for getting to know your students?

PRE-GAME TIP #12: BE TRUSTWORTHY AND CONSISTENT

Consistency builds trust. Ever since I was five years old, the milkshake machine at McDonald's has been broken. I know that if I'm going to go tomorrow, the attendant will say, "The machine is broken, no milkshake." I'm currently thirty-seven years old, and that machine is STILL broken. Conversely, if I go to Chick-fil-A and ask for fifteen hot sauces and four honey mustards for just five nuggets, they are going to say, "My pleasure," and give me all of the sauces. One of my friends said, "Chick-fil-A is so consistent that I don't even check my bag for the correct order. I *trust* that it's going to be accurate." Both of these places are extremely consistent, positively and negatively. We can positively expect that Chick-fil-A will give us the sauces, while, on the flipside, the McDonald's milkshake machine is still broken. It's kind of funny when you think about it. Our classes are similar. One student will be on point in one class, and then be the complete opposite in another. Why? Consistency. If the expectations are set, and the teacher is consistent in what he or she asks students to do and holds them to that standard, students will respond to that. If I am consistent in not setting the bar high with my expectations, then students will respond accordingly. If I know I can cut up in your class, I will. Building trust starts on day one. Whatever issues you want to keep to a minimum, start firm and be relentless with those expectations from the get-go. You can always lighten up later.

This was probably one of the most challenging concepts because it requires a great amount of discipline and really holding yourself and students accountable to the norms and structure of your class. The key here is to follow through with the things that you want to happen in your class. If you said no cell phones, then whatever consequence or action that you said would happen if a student is caught with one must take place. As I've told you, students are extremely aware, and, just like any other person, even adults, they look for loopholes and ways to slide by. Students will try you. Be consistent in what you say and do. By being consistent, after a while, they will understand that your expectations and structures are not going to be lowered. An additional piece of advice is to prioritize your battles. You may not want to go toe-to-toe on everything. How much time is spent holding the line on something that really doesn't impact their ability to learn and your ability to teach? What battles are for compliance, and what battles are for a purpose? This will make teaching a lot easier for you in your class.

Practice: Identify one thing that you want to be a non-negotiable in your classroom and commit to holding yourself and your students accountable to it. Also, think about a contingency plan in case your non-negotiable is broken.

PRE-GAME TIP #13: ACHIEVE TECHNICAL MASTERY

Technical mastery is another way to build trust because students trust that you are skilled and an expert of your content. Just think about it, why would I hire a water polo coach to teach me how to become a basketball player? It doesn't make sense. I have several coaches that I have hired to help me grow personally and professionally. I have a relationship coach, Ashley, and a business and communications coach, Mel B. I hired them both because they are experts in their fields. I trust that they will bring forth the necessary skills to support and challenge me to grow in these specific areas. This same expertise applies to teaching. We want to build our skill set and master the art of teaching.

Technical mastery means learning the superior skills of effective teaching. Effective teaching will contribute to your culture and learning environment. You want to engage students from the moment they enter the door until the bell rings. My motto was: We work from bell to bell. *"But how, Sway, how do I master the art of teaching?"* I will be honest, it was challenging to learn, but I want to give you a few tips to help you improve your skills as a teacher. Great teaching also will eliminate a lot of behavioral issues in your class because students will be so invested in what you are selling each day that they won't have time to get off task. Here are a few of the things that I did to improve my craft as a teacher:

- **Have a growth mindset.** You are going to experience a plethora of emotions as you move throughout the year. And, at some point, you will fail. A key pillar to accepting this failure is having a growth mindset. A growth mindset is about examining your efforts and identifying what you can learn from the challenges and how to do better moving forward. Becoming a great teacher does not happen overnight. It's through consistent learning and effort. In order to succeed in the long run, you're going to have to fail from time to time.

- **Build your content knowledge.** Learn and study your content. One of the best things you can do is dive deep into your content and be well-prepared. Study your text. In math, we often promote "doing the math," and, in English, we recommend thoroughly reading and reviewing your text.

- **Attend professional learning and development classes.** Normally, your school district or school will offer several professional learning experiences to help you improve your craft. GO! This is free training to help you improve your content knowledge and pedagogy. I will give you a prime example. There is one teacher who attended every professional learning class that the district offered. She had taught pretty much for her entire career and interviewed for a job as an English advisor. Other people interviewed and had plenty more experience, but she got the job because she had grown in her content knowledge. Attend every career building course that you can. It's free, and you get better as a teacher. I was able to become an educational consultant because I went to all the trainings. I'm addicted to learning, and that's what gives you an edge as a professional.

- **Observe other strong teachers to learn effective teaching practices.** Go learn from other strong teachers! I would advise you to be selective in terms of who you observe. The teachers that I chose to observe had results to match their strong reputations. I wanted to learn from the best. Harry Wong, an educational guru and author of *The First Days of School* (highly recommend that read), says to steal everything. That is exactly what I did. I had a team of teachers that supported me in the first year, and I would constantly be in their rooms observing their practices. I would borrow their styles, then remix it and make it my own. By observing strong teachers, it allows you to know two things: One, it's possible to effectively manage a classroom and provide an environment where strong teaching and learning can take place. Two, it helps you identify teaching moves that you may want to add to your repertoire.

- **Find a coach to support and challenge you to improve your practice.** Every good player has a coach. Coaching and mentoring are very different. (We will dive deeper into mentoring in the next section.) Coaching is focused on improving performance. You need to have someone who pushes you to your edge so you can continue to improve in your teaching practice. As I stated earlier, I have two coaches, and I pay them to keep me uncomfortable and hold me accountable. Having a coach can make you feel vulnerable because you are putting yourself on display, but don't fret. My teaching practice was a hot mess, and because of coaching and willingness to receive feedback, I improved bit by bit each year.

Practice: Which commitments are you going to make to move you toward technical mastery?

Commit to at least two of the action steps above and write about what you learned from your action step.

Action Step #1:	What I learned about myself from implementation:

Action Step #2:	What I learned about myself from implementation:

Action Step #3:	What I learned about myself from implementation:

PRE-GAME PLAN TIP #14: FIND A MENTOR

Teaching is one of those professions where you will learn on the job. As we discussed in the previous section, a coach and mentor are completely different. A coach focuses on improving your performance, while a mentor provides you with support. (And, trust me, you are going to need it.) According to the article "New Teachers Need Professional and Emotional Support," teaching is an emotional profession, and the emotional state of teachers directly impacts students' ability to behave and learn. Two things the article specifically touched on that a new teacher will need are effective professional and emotional support, and non-judgmental understanding and patience. This is where your mentor comes in. You will absolutely need one. Keep in mind they are here to help you grow into this new role, so please don't be afraid to seek help and ask a lot of questions.

A great mentor will support you in adapting to the school climate and culture, and this new line of work. With all of the emotions and challenges that may arise, you'll want to have someone who can support you in mitigating some of the challenges.

More than likely, they have already experienced them and can help you out.

According to INcompassing Education, approximately 50 percent of teachers leave the profession within the first five years. Teaching can be stressful with all the moving parts, which is why it is essential to find a solid mentor, preferably at your school. Additionally, a mentor can provide you with practical tips and strategies, as well as logistics to navigate teaching. For example, they can teach you how to build an effective lesson plan. There are certain aspects of the role you aren't going to know, and that's okay. But I'm sure there is someone in the building who can help and support you in this new role.

Personally, I wanted mentors who were familiar with my specific content. That way, they could help me with some of the nuances. I also sought out positive, growth-minded individuals. I did not want to learn from someone who found the negative as to why certain things weren't possible. I was fortunate in that I had not one but three mentors that really took me under their wing and showed me the lay of the land. Thanks to their hard work, I felt well-prepared and was able to lead and support others as I moved on throughout my career.

Practice: Identify the attributes you value in a mentor (e.g., strong results, content-specific, good leadership style, etc.) and list them below. Then, find a mentor who has those qualities.

PRE-GAME TIP #15: WHAT IS YOUR F.L.Y.?

So, I'm sure you are asking, what is your F.L.Y.? F.L.Y. stand for the Fashionable Look for You. As discussed earlier in the book, it's important that you own your story and really bring your authentic self. That can also be displayed via your fashion and style. As you think about the first day of school, keep in mind that you don't get a second chance to make a first impression. I want you to ask yourself: What is the message that I want to send to my students on day one?

This may sound corny, but get your "first day of school" outfit ready! Do you remember when you went school shopping and you were looking for the right shoes, shirts, and accessories to be "fly" on the first day of school? I remember I would lay my outfit out the day before from top to bottom. I need you to think about that now. Dress is important in terms of the message we send to our students. As I progressed throughout each year, the first day outfit had to be "fly" and professional, simply because I wanted to set the tone and exude a professional demeanor. One of the reasons I chose to dress up for the first few weeks is because, at the time, I looked extremely young, and I wanted to make a clear divide between friend and teacher.

I'm not saying that you need to break the bank, but you definitely want to show your "executive presence." That term comes from the book *Executive Presence* by Sarah Ann Hewlett. In it, she states, "*Your appearance is the medium in which your message is conveyed.*" So, it's critical that you make a strong first impression in order to effectively communicate your message.

Here are a few more tips from the book:

- **Be groomed, neat, and polished.** A neat appearance shows that you have put effort into yourself, which will send the message that you will put effort into your work. It gives off the vibe that you are committed to yourself and gives the perception of confidence and credibility.
- **Find your own professional style.** I'm not saying that you need to be dressed in a three-piece suit, but you will want to find your own

unique style. This took some time for me to figure out. My style was either khakis, polos, and Sperry boat shoes, or a nice pair of dress slacks and a button-down dress shirt. I was a super active teacher, so I needed comfortable shoes but wanted to stay in a professional look. Another educator I knew wore business casual and sneakers, but that was his style.

- **Dress appropriately for your audience.** This one is key because, again, first impressions are essential. It may not be a good idea to wear what you would wear to a club or night out with your boo. As I stated, I personally like to dress up to set a clear divide between being a teacher and a friend because I looked so young. I would recommend professional dress for the first weeks.

- **Ask a mentor for feedback if you are unsure of what you selected.** If you are unsure about the appropriateness of your outfit, ask a trusted colleague, mentor, or friend to give you feedback.

What's the style that embodies you? What is your first day of school outfit? What is the message you want to convey to your students through your attire?

PRE-GAME TIP #16: DO A WALKTHROUGH OF DAY ONE

When I played college basketball, on game day, we would do a walkthrough. A walkthrough is a one-hour pre-game practice to prepare you for the actual game. We would run through our plays, review the other team's offensive and defensive schemes, and put up a few shots. The practices weren't super intense because the sole purpose was to warm us up and get us prepared for the actual game and tip-off. You want to do the same thing as you prepare for day one of teaching. This is an opportunity to "walk through" your first day. How will you run your plays? How will you prepare for students' offensive and defensive schemes? How will you get your reps and put up your shots?

I recommend making sure that your own personal home court (i.e., your classroom) is set up the way you would like, then determine if there are any components you need to add. Remember how we created a run of show in the earlier portion of the book? This "walkthrough" is a pre-game warm-up of your "run of show." Check your technology, your desks. Are your copies ready, activities prepared? One year, I did my walkthrough and realized that I forgot to number my desks, so I had to take care of it that day. Or once my technology was off, and I needed to purchase an additional cord for it to display properly. Additionally, practice your opening day speech over and over. This is essential to making a strong first impression and solidifying your presence on the first day of school. One teacher that I worked with had some challenges with classroom management for several years. However, when we worked together to prepare him for day one, the classroom was more manageable that year. He practiced his speech continuously—he wrote it out, practiced in the mirror, called me on the phone for feedback, all to ensure that he was ready.

Practice: Complete a walkthrough a few days before school starts. Also, practice your speech in and out of class. If you really want to push yourself, invite another teacher to give you feedback.

PRE-GAME TIP #17: PRACTICE YOUR ROUTINES THROUGH ACTIVITIES

The first week, a large part of your job will consist of getting to know your students and establishing a strong culture. Find activities where you can learn more about your students *and* practice your run of show, procedures, and routines. Even though I knew that I did not have actual math problems for my students to do on the first day of school, I had activities prepared where they also learned my routines and procedures. For example, I knew that every day that they came in the classroom they would be picking up a Do Now activity from the table, so I had their "getting to know you" sheet set up in that spot so that they could practice and rehearse the actual routine that they would be doing all year.

Return to your "run of show." What activities do you want to create to provide opportunities for your students to practice these activities? Identify which activities you will be utilizing to practice your routine. Below is a run of show template. Place your activity in each block.

Time Stamp	**Activity**	**Practice Activity**
Pre-game (prior to bell ringing)— 2 minutes into class	Gather instructional materials (sharpen pencils, grab calculators, etc.)	
Bell rings—5 minutes	Complete **Do Now** and complete pre-game activities	
2–3 minutes	Recap **Do Now**	
1–2 minutes	Lesson intro— connect to prior knowledge	
30 minutes	Lesson activities (meat of the lesson)	
3–5 minutes	Synthesis, summary, closure of the lesson	
5 minutes	Exit ticket and cool down	

"CONSISTENCY IS THE FOUNDATION OF TRUST."

—ROY T. BENNETT

PART IV

GETTING YOUR INSTRUCTIONAL "GAME" RIGHT

GAME TIP #18: BE CONSISTENT AND CONNECT

CONGRATULATIONS! YOU MADE it through day one, and I'm pretty sure you smashed it. The game really gets started after tip-off. The first quarter is essential to a strong start to your game. How do you continue your momentum of establishing yourself as a trustworthy, credible, and knowledgeable teacher? The keyword is consistency. Today, you laid the groundwork for several of our pre-game tips. You may be asking, *What do consistency and connection have to do with high-quality teaching?* I thought the same thing. *I'm here to teach math, why do these other things matter?* Consistency and connection are the foundation for effectively teaching your content. Without these, teaching does not happen.

You know your "run of show" and what you want to take place in your class, but the foundation of your house will be determined by your consistent execution and holding your students accountable. Students will almost certainly try to push your boundaries to see how firm you are with your expectations. For example, I had a strict policy about cell phones. I told my students, "I do not want to see it or hear it in class. This is our time to get mathletically fit!" I told them if I saw a cell phone, I'd take it from them—even if it was an accident. I understand accidents do happen. However, I wanted to emphasize the importance of ensuring a cell phone is silenced while in class. On the third day of school, a student's phone went off, and, to set a strong example, I seized it. I immediately felt some uneasiness when I took the phone, but I knew the key was to remain calm and adhere to my policies and routines. By doing this, I was sending a clear message that I would not only talk the talk, I would walk the walk.

Consider that consistency is the first half, but the other half is continuing to build connections and establishing relationships with your students. When I say relationships, I don't mean that you should be your student's friend. In Harry Wong's book, *The First Days of School*, he states when you are someone's friend, they expect favors. When you don't, they may say "I don't like you," versus establishing setting a clear line as a role model and someone that your students can respect. As I told you earlier, because I looked very young when I first started teaching, I had to be firm and consistent to avoid giving my students the wrong impression. The first two days, I would provide different activities where they had the space to tell me about themselves, and often I would participate in these activities to share about myself as well. (Remember, you still want to adhere to your routines and do these activities through your own procedures and routines. Do not abandon your classroom management plan for these activities.)

Here's a quote that's fitting for this very topic: *"True learning starts with vulnerability."* Understand that the relationship is just not one-sided. Students want to see that you are a human being as well. Establishing strong relationships is an essential component to having a solid school year. If you are unable to connect with your audience, hear me when I say that it's going to be more challenging for them to learn with you. Without strong relationships and culture, learning will not happen. People respond to authentic people, and if you have strong relationships, students will go the extra mile for you. As a coach, I often see this pattern in classes: a teacher will have the best content knowledge, but the students are disengaged because there is no relationship.

In order to foster connections and consistency in your classroom, feel free to utilize some of these suggestions. You can always try googling, too. You may want to look for grade-specific activities, as high school activities will be different than those created for elementary students.

My connection activity: I would ask the students to pick five numbers (math class). Each number would represent a fun fact about themselves. I'd ask the students to put their most important number in the middle and explain why they chose that number as their most important. They could color it, decorate it, or do whatever they would like. After we finished the activity, I would urge them to share in groups amongst each other. Then, each person would stand up in front of the class and share one of their numbers and a cool fact about themselves.

Practice: What procedures, routines, and policies do you want to emphasize during the first weeks/months of school? What's your strategy for keeping yourself consistent? Also, identify the activities you will use for the first day of school to build relationships with your students. For additional tools to help you connect with your students, visit www.mentalfitzness.com/resources.

"HIGH-QUALITY INSTRUCTION IS ANALOGOUS TO A HEALTHY DIET. IT IS THE KEY INDICATOR OF THE EDUCATIONAL FITNESS OF A SCHOOL."

—ANDREA FITZGERALD

GAME TIP #19: WHAT'S IN YOUR SANDWICH?

"The teacher is the most important in-school factor in student achievement."
(Ladson-Billings, 1999)

"The student is the most important variable in the learning equation."
(Murphy, 2013)

YOU ARE STARTING to build relationships and establishing a strong culture, and now it's time to roll out your grade-level content. You have your textbook, you have studied the material, but how will you effectively share this information with your students? What am I talking about? Your instructional framework. According to Angela Grant (aka the Turnaround Coach), *"Struggling schools most likely do not have strong instructional systems, so student success is often left to chance or individual teacher talent, which is not evenly distributed high poverty schools.*" Strong instruction is analogous to a healthy diet. Three essential pieces that contribute to being physically fit are mindset, healthy diet, and exercise. Fitness is my jam, and I have the mindset to get up and work out five days a week. However, I sometimes eat unhealthy foods, which impacts my mental and physical health even though I'm going hard in the gym most days of the week. Research has shown that 60 percent of our health is tied to what we eat. That same idea can be applied to instruction. That's how impactful a strong teacher with solid instruction is to a school. It's essential for a healthy school, and, most importantly, it's essential for our students.

When I first started teaching, I would read the textbook on Sundays, jot down some notes, and I thought I could just come in the classroom, teach, and voilà—my students would learn. That approach didn't work out. They weren't learning much of anything. That's because I didn't understand the importance of a teaching framework. A framework is an essential supporting structure of a building, vehicle, or object. You want to think of your teaching framework similarly. You can either use a template or notes to follow a framework. Personally, I was a fan of annotating my lessons versus a lesson plan; however, it still followed the framework. Having a framework will support you in rolling out a lesson. There are several you can use, and some are listed below. One of my administrators shared the "Learning by Design" framework with me and that was my bread and butter. You may be asking yourself, *What is an instructional framework?* I'm going to break down that concept and provide you with additional ideas. You want to think of your framework as a sandwich, and you want to have the right ingredients for an effective lesson.

Additionally, your curriculum often provides you with guidance on how to facilitate the content as you think about the meat of the lesson.

ROOK/E

The Sandwich
Instructional Framework

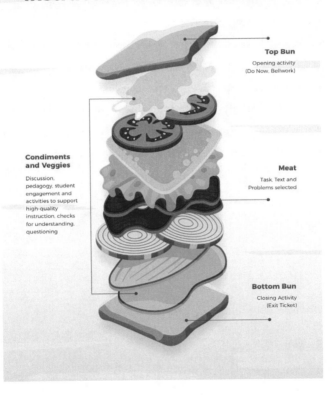

Top Bun

Opening activity
(Do Now, Bellwork)

**Condiments
and Veggies**

Discussion,
pedagogy, student
engagement and
activities to support
high-quality
instruction, checks
for understanding,
questioning

Meat

Task, Text and
Problems selected

Bottom Bun

Closing Activity
(Exit Ticket)

- Top of the bun: opening a lesson
- Meat: content, engagement, and activities to support high-quality instruction
- Bottom of the bun: closing a lesson

I'd also like to add that a strong closing and opening makes all the difference in preparing a lesson. As a teacher, you want to ensure that the right activities align with the big idea of the lesson. Visit mentalfitzness.com/resources for additional instructional frameworks to support you in teaching.

Practice: What teaching framework will you utilize to facilitate your lesson? List a run of show for teaching a lesson.

GAME TIP #20: MEAL PREP

About a month ago, I was having trouble sticking to my diet. I felt like I had no self-control. If I saw chips, I ate them. Candy...gobble, gobble! I felt like I could not pull it together. Well, one day, I decided to pack my lunch and any snacks I wanted to eat. That day, I stayed true to eating healthy. I surprised myself and wanted to give myself a huge pat on the back. After a moment of reflection, I kept thinking, *This day really worked out for me. Why?* And the answer was quite simple and obvious: I prepared my meals and snacks. Therefore, I already knew what I was going to eat for the entire day, and it was easy to adhere to the plan. How does this relate to teaching, you may ask? If great instruction is analogous to a healthy diet, then we have to prepare the meals that we are going to cook. *"How, Sway? How do we do that?"* This is where the lesson plan comes in. You need to have a clear idea of how you're going to engage with students and the content each day.

I'm going to be real—I wasn't a fan of lesson planning once I was in the game for a minute. What I really despised was the template. However, first starting out, it was very helpful because it provided me with a framework of how to facilitate the lesson. I'm not knocking templates, but what I found to be more important was knowing exactly what I would be doing every day, then referring to my notes for the specific details. I'm not telling you which way to do it, but just like you have a run of show for management, you may also want to consider having a run of show for the rollout of your lesson, except you want it to be content-specific.

Additionally, I would recommend planning with others. It's powerful to have conversations about the content. When I was the new kid on the block, these planning conversations were invaluable. One: I got guidance on how to facilitate my lessons, and two: I received feedback on adjustments that I could make to my current plans. Find a team of teachers to collaborate with immediately!

Having a strong lesson plan also eliminates behavioral and classroom management issues. When I first started teaching, I would read the section and try to stick to the book without taking the time to do the math or even internalizing the material. The lessons often fell flat, and classroom management went off the rails because I didn't have a tight plan for how everything would flow. As you continue to read the next few tips, I will share my strategies for how I prepared my lessons. Here are some things to consider when you are "meal prepping" or preparing your lessons.

- Start with the end in mind. What's your objective for the lesson? What do you want students to know and be able to do at the end of the lesson?
- What are your opening and closing activities?
- What activities, tasks, problems, or text will you utilize to meet those objectives?

- Check for student understanding. Are the kids in the car? Assess reliably and efficiently. Where are your checks for understanding?
- Anticipate the house falling down. Where could students potentially have misconceptions? How will you adjust?
- What engagement strategies will you implement?

Practice: Based on your sandwich (i.e., your instructional framework), what's your plan for meal prepping for an upcoming lesson? Is there a lesson plan template that makes sense for you? Are you going to use lesson annotations? Is there a designated day that you want to plan? Do you want to plan multiple lessons at a time?

GAME TIP #21: WHAT'S YOUR TARGET? IDENTIFY THE OBJECTIVE OF YOUR LESSON

What are the things you do to prepare for a trip? I'm sure you pack your bags, book your hotel and lodging, get your homelife situated, and determine how you are going to get there. Is it better to fly or drive? If we were going to Hawaii, we would know that a car would not be sufficient to take us to our destination. However, what do you do before all of that? You determine your destination. Where are you going? You want to consider the same thing with your lesson.

When I was in my teacher education program, one of our assignments was to do a model lesson and share it with the class. The topic of my lesson was the Pythagorean Theorem. I planned all of these activities and had this amazing PowerPoint presentation, but my professor asked, "What did you want them to understand as a result of this lesson?" Did I want them to find the hypotenuse? Did I want them to solve real-world problems? I was not clear on the objective of my lesson. I wanted them to know more about the Pythagorean Theorem, but I did not have outcomes and targets that students needed to achieve by the end of the lesson. If you have ever been to a football game, it was almost as if I was tailgating in the parking lot but never made it into the actual arena.

Without having a clear objective, the lesson can fall flat, and classroom management issues can sneak in. Most importantly, it impacts student achievement, because without knowing where you are going, you can't do the right things to get there.

Start with a target of what students need to be able to do at the end of the lesson, then start the planning process based on knowing that these activities will get you to that target. Most times, your curriculum will provide you with the objectives of the lesson and guidance on how to meet those outcomes. As we move through the next few tips, you will gain guidance on how to align your activities to the objective of the lesson.

Practice: Identify the objective(s) and outcomes of your lesson.

GAME TIP #22: COMPLETE THE TASK AS IF YOU ARE A STUDENT PRIOR TO PLANNING

Several years ago, I was tutoring a student in eighth-grade math. I was an algebra teacher, so I thought to myself, *How hard could this be?* We were working on finding the slope of a line, which I had taught a million times. I started the session, and we worked through the lesson to build his knowledge of how to find the slope, but it was done in a different way than I was used to. The lesson was utilizing transparencies to build the concept of slope, which I had never taught. At that moment, I got so anxious. I turned beet red inside. Here I am, the tutor, the "expert," and I had no idea how to find the slope this way. I played it off and told him, "We are going to skip this one."

It's funny now, but why did the house fall down in my session? It was because I hadn't completed the math or task from the student's viewpoint. I did not know what to expect that day, and it showed. Therefore, my student did not get what he needed that day. I would highly recommend that, prior to planning your lesson, you complete the task that you want students to do throughout the lesson. There are multiple benefits to this approach.

First, you will be able to anticipate where students may have some challenges and think through how you will support them. This is so important as you consider that your lessons will not always go as planned, and sometimes students may not understand your "perfectly planned lesson." This caught me up several times. I would come in with this well-prepared lesson and have no idea what to do when they didn't understand. It is beneficial to be prepared for those moments so you can make proper adjustments. Let me preface by saying that you may not be prepared for all of the misconceptions, but completing the task helps you be better prepared to address them.

Secondly, you will have a much deeper understanding of the content, which will paint the picture of an expert in front of your students. This builds a high level of credibility that you are knowledgeable and know what you are talking about.

As you complete the task, start informally identifying what the big idea of the task is. This will help you as you start the actual planning process. It's that simple: complete the task prior to planning.

Practice: I will say it again.... COMPLETE THE TASK PRIOR TO PLANNING. Now, answer the following questions: What's the big idea of the task(s) that I just completed? Which parts of the lesson were challenging for me? How might my students struggle?

GAME TIP #23: WHAT IS THE MEAT OF YOUR SANDWICH?

After you have completed your task or read your task as a student, revisit your objective and think about the content, teacher moves, and student engagement strategies that will complement said objective. If you think about it, what makes a sandwich so tasty? It's the stuff in the middle—veggies, meat, cheese—these are the things that make for a solid lesson, just like that sandwich. Remember, you always want to keep the objective and standard as the North Star for your instructional decisions. How you structure the meat of your lesson sets the stage for student learning. Richard Elmore's instructional core highlights three essential components of solid instruction: content, teacher, and students. However, we will apply the analogy of a healthy and meaty instructional sandwich for our purposes.

Content—Do you have the right vehicle?

Do you have the right meat in your sandwich? Do you have grade-level content for students to engage in? I would strongly suggest utilizing a highly aligned curriculum to the standards in your respective state, depending on your state standards. One, it's an equitable practice for students to have access to the right content, regardless of what neighborhood they are from. Two, they often provide guidance on what instructional moves may be beneficial to your students. And three, "The task of the lesson sets the ceiling for how far one can go." You want to think of aligned curriculum as the springboard to planning an effective lesson. You can be making all of the right moves, but if you don't have the right content on the table for students, you may fall short in meeting the demand of the standards. Imagine saying I want to go to the moon, but I'm going to get there with a boat. You can be navigating the boat seamlessly, but you are not moving toward the moon. The content is the vehicle to get us to our goal or destination.

Side note: I attended the Boston Winter Standards Institute, which is based on introducing you and helping you learn about standards. When I entered the room, the keynote speaker had an opening slide that read *RTFS*. I was confused and curious about what the heck that actually meant. The keynote speaker walked onto the stage and said, "RTFS—read the f$#&ing standard!" *Wow, welcome to Boston*, I thought.

She continued to explain that it's important to start with the standard or your state objectives before you begin to plan your lesson, select your task, figure out student engagement moves, or even your

---

pedagogical moves. The standard is the "North Star" of what you want to accomplish in your class, and the content is the "vehicle" to get you there. So, if you remember one thing from this section: RTFS!

She continued to explain that it's important to start with the standard or your state objectives before you begin to plan your lesson, select your task, figure out student engagement moves, or even your pedagogical moves. The standard is the "North Star" of what you want to accomplish in your class, and the content is the "vehicle" to get you there. So, if you remember one thing from this section: RTFS!

PART V

PRIME TIME PLAYER PEDAGOGY (PTP)

PTP PEDAGOGY—LET'S MAKE THE MOVES

DICK VITALE IS a well-known sports broadcaster who has different terms and slogans he uses to highlight the unique skill sets of different players. There are two that I want to share with you. I want you to encompass both of these as a teacher. The first is Diaper Dandy, which is a sensational freshman, since you are a rookie in the game. The second is we want you to make PTPer Pedagogy. A PTPer is a Prime Time Player, which, in education, we are going to slate as an effective teacher. You have the capacity to become a PTPer, even in your first year as a Diaper Dandy.

If you have the right meat for your sandwich, you'll want to ensure that you are making the right moves with it. One of the tools that I often use as a coach is the Instructional Practice Guide, which was created by Student Achievement Partners. It provides guidance on what is considered high-quality, standards-aligned instruction. I promise you it's not that deep or complex. The research-based key actions provided are essential to high-quality instruction. It is a great tool to utilize when preparing your lessons, or even when receiving content-specific feedback.

GAME TIP #24: TOP BUN OF THE SANDWICH = OPENING ACTIVITY

The top layer of the bun is considered to be the opening activity (or "Do Now"). If you recall, Do Now refers to a bell work activity that students can engage in upon entering the door. You almost want to think of this as an opportunity to either connect prior knowledge or hook them into the lesson. When I first started teaching, I would often walk into my class and just start the lesson without building interest or knowledge, and the students did not connect to the lesson. Also, with your opening activity, you may want to think about knowing your audience and identify and make adjustments to the task or question to make it somewhat interesting. You want to ensure that your opening activity is meaningful and worthwhile. It's also a great way to gather evidence of what students actually know, which can be missed if you jump right into the lesson without a warm-up.

You want to think of the opening activity as a warm-up before the actual workout or "meat" of the lesson. The question you want to ask yourself is: What is the intent of the opening activity? For example, my opening activity was often the same each day. I created an End of Course quiz with five questions each day. Oftentimes, I would adjust my opening activity based on what information that I needed from students that day. Sometimes I would start with an open-ended question to solidify understanding for students and get a pulse on what information students already knew.

Another benefit of having a strong opening activity is you set the tone for your class. Just like the first few days of school are essential, the first five to seven minutes of your class are important as well. I have seen several teachers lose control of their class because they had nothing for the students to do right away, which could potentially give students the idea that there is no structure.

Here are some guiding questions to help you build your opening activity:

- What's the objective of the lesson?
- What opening activity will I utilize to introduce this concept?
- What is the purpose of my opening activity? How does this connect to the meat of my lesson?
- How will I monitor what students understand from the opening activity?
- How long will this task be?

Practice: Commit to having an opening activity for each one of your lessons.... ERRDAY! After selecting the opening activity for your lessons, identify the purpose of the activity and how it connects to your lesson.

"IF YOU CAN'T EXPLAIN IT SIMPLY, YOU DON'T UNDERSTAND IT WELL ENOUGH."

—ALBERT EINSTEIN

GAME TIP #25: PROVIDE CLEAR COMMUNICATION AND EXPLANATION

I OBSERVED A first-year teacher's classroom several weeks ago. This man knew the content; however, his class was all over the place. It was almost as if he were talking to himself out of a 20+ student class. He asked the students to do a problem in their groups. As he circulated around the room, he would re-teach every student the concept. Why, though? Why were students disengaged and not interested in what he was talking about? Why didn't they understand when they finally had an opportunity to attempt the problem by themselves? Obviously, there were some classroom management issues, but at the core of it all, the explanation was unclear. Students did not understand what the teacher communicated prior to releasing them to work.

I'm not sharing this story in judgment or shade—I've been that teacher too. I'm sure you know your content, but it's another thing to know how to effectively communicate and transfer that knowledge to another person. For example, I knew how to solve two-step equations. That was the very first lesson I taught, but the kids did not understand at all because I did not know how to communicate it in a clear, concise way.

Effective communication begins with knowing your audience and making the concept relatable. Practice your explanations to ensure that they are clear and can be easily understood by students. When I taught functions, since I was in high school, I knew that dating was a big topic of conversation, so I related the concepts of relations and functions to dating. What you want to ensure is that you don't oversimplify the concept, but you want to relate it to everyday life in some way. Visual models can also be more effective than just talking about a complex idea, so keep that in mind in case you need to show versus tell.

Analogies and stories are my jam. I use them in just about every time I coach, consult, tutor, and many other areas of my business. About six months ago, I participated in this program, the Business of

Speaking and Coaching, because I thought I wanted to be a motivational speaker. What I learned in that program was invaluable. The leader of the program, Kendall Ficklin, stated that the key to communication is stories—80 percent story, 20 percent principle. Teaching isn't totally 80 percent. However, the important part is tying the key information of your lessons into stories or ideas that are relatable to your students.

Practice: Review your current lesson and identify a piece of the lesson that requires a clear explanation. Script out the key ideas and your explanation to students. Practice your explanation with a colleague or mentor and receive feedback.

Lesson title and objective:	
Key idea of the lesson:	

Which is the most important piece of the lesson?	
Script out your explanation for this piece of the lesson. Does the curriculum provide guidance on explaining key points?	
Practice with a colleague, coach, mentor, or friend. Jot down notes on the feedback that you got from your practice partner(s).	

GAME TIP #26: CHECKS FOR UNDERSTANDING: ARE THE KIDS IN THE CAR?

Does everyone understand? You get it? You got it? Any questions? These are decent questions to ask in class, but they provide you with no evidence of what students actually know. Let's take a road trip. Say we are traveling to Two-Step Equation County. How did we even get there? In this lesson, my first stop on the trip was supposed to be one-step equations. However, because I started in the middle of the year, I did not know where to start, so I asked the students this powerful question: "Does everyone know how to solve one-step equations?" It seemed fairly easy to me. All of the students in my class responded with a resounding "YES." And I believed it, so I kept on teaching. Little did I know that it would all come crashing down at the end of the lesson when students had to solve the two-step equations on their own.

When I finally looked at their work, I was dazed and confused. The kids did not arrive to the destination of the lesson, which was understanding how to solve two-step equations fluently and accurately. The reason they did not understand was because I did not check for understanding to ensure they "got it" as we moved throughout the lesson.

I went to a faculty meeting the following week, and Ms. Webb, the vice principal, was facilitating a session on checks for understanding. Her recommendation was that, just like a good driver checks their rearview mirror every 2–3 minutes, you want to do the same in your own class. This was a game changer for me in terms of PTP Pedagogy. You want to have intentional checkpoints throughout the lesson to monitor the progress of students going to your destination. Hence my analogy, are the kids in the car? Every so often, you want to gather evidence and determine: Are you still in the car? Are you with me? You want to have actual work to show what students know and check on their thinking processes. I would use small white dry erase boards so I could see the work firsthand, versus a student simply lucking up on an answer.

An essential piece of checks for understanding is planning for them. If you are considering the destination that you want students to arrive to at the end of the lesson, you want to identify the essential checkpoints throughout the lesson that are necessary to arrive there. You almost want to reverse engineer the essential skills required to achieve mastery. As each task in the lesson becomes more complex, you want to identify the key understanding that students need to know from the task and anticipate where students may struggle or have misconceptions. Also, determine how you will perform this check. I used whiteboards, questioning, and additional tools.

I like to think of misconceptions as identifying where there could be a car crash in the lesson. As you think about misconceptions, you want to also think about adjustments that you will make in case the kids are not in the car. How will you get them back on the road and in the car when it breaks down? It helps to be prepared for those moments and have questions or scaffolds to support them when the time comes. I personally liked the whiteboards because I liked seeing the students' thinking process. Visit mentalfitzness.com/resources to review additional resources and ideas for checking for understanding.

Practice: Review your current lesson that you will be implementing. As you look through each problem or task, identify the big idea and what students need to know.

Big Idea:

CFU (How and what):

Big Idea:

CFU (How and what):

Big Idea:

CFU (How and what):

"I HEAR AND I FORGET. I SEE AND I REMEMBER. I DO AND I UNDERSTAND."

—CONFUCIUS

GAME TIP #27: HOW WILL STUDENTS EAT THE SANDWICH? (STUDENT ENGAGEMENT)

AS A COACH, I've been in several classrooms, and all of the pieces are there except hearing from one of our most valuable assets: our students. You have been a master chef and created your sandwich, and now you want to think about how the students will eat the sandwich (i.e., engage with your content). Do you want them to have a whole group discussion? In pairs? In groups of three? Individually? Do you want to bring in technology? In regard to engagement, you want to ask yourself: How do I make this lesson come ALIVE? How do I add some flavor and make this content exciting for students? This is totally up to you, but research has shown that students can often benefit from collaborating with one another. According to Cornell University, *"educational experiences that are active, social, contextual, engaging, and student-owned lead to deeper learning."*

You want to provide opportunities for students to use their voice in your classroom. Often, if you have a strongly aligned curriculum, they provide tips and engagement strategies to help you identify some of the best places in the lesson for student collaboration. This was challenging because when I first started teaching, I did a lot of whole group teaching where I was at the board and students were in rows. I did not have great classroom management, so it often felt scary to allow them to be in groups.

The other half of student engagement is teaching students how to interact in groups. I would recommend having students practice how to engage in groups ahead of time. The train can go off the track very easily without strong classroom management and solid routines in place. I'd often tell my students, "I understand that what is going on this weekend is important, but I want to hear you talking about math!" The engagement doesn't stop right there, though. Monitoring the progress, circulating, and checking in occasionally is essential to success with engagement strategies. Utilize the student conversations as a way to see if the kids are in the car, but also gather evidence in terms of how you want to guide the lesson. I would also recommend having a few back pocket questions to ask students as you circulate around the classroom. Remember, this goes back to knowing the path you want students to take and understanding the big idea of where you want them to be at the end of the lesson.

You also want to select the engagement strategy that is most appropriate for the task/text that you are working on. There are times when whole group instruction is effective. However, with whole group instruction, it's important that your explanations are clear and engaging. When I say that, I mean you don't want to be the only one talking in the room. Think of instruction as a dance. Sometimes you lead, and sometimes your students lead, but we are all going to the same place!

Find a tool! I have been in relationship school for the past three months, and it's pretty challenging stuff. However, I have seen myself grow and make some shifts because they provide tools to support us. I have a toolkit that I can utilize for targeted situations. As you think about engagement, you want to find a tool or routine to support you in effective student engagement. Protocols and routines are great tools because they provide a research-based framework to support you in providing an engaging environment for students. Below are some tools that I often used in my class, and they are money in the bank. Please feel free to utilize them at your leisure. Please share on Instagram @mentalfitzness any tools that you use!

Visit www.mentalfitzness.com/resources for a few effective engagement strategies.

Practice: Consider this: I want you to think about a lecture that you have attended that has been boring. List what made this experience uninteresting.

Now, flip it and think about the best classroom experience or presentation that you have ever attended. What was exciting about it? Why do you remember it?

As you consider those components for engagement planning in your class, what attributes will you add to your class to make it engaging for your students? Review a current lesson and determine where you will include these strategies.

GAME TIP #28: TEACHER PIZAZZ—SELL YOUR CONTENT

I've visited over 1,000 classrooms to observe math. One classroom sticks out in my mind. The students had a mutual respect for the teacher. They were compliant and completed the assigned tasks. It was almost as if they were robots. They were quiet and well behaved, but there was rarely any interaction between the teacher and students. The energy was somewhat stale.

Conversely, I went to another teacher's classroom. The students were eager to answer every question. The teacher posed a question, and hands flew up! They were engaged and hung on to the teacher's every word. This second class I visited, I was blown away and super hyped up to do math when I left. I stepped out of the classroom, and the coach told me that a large portion of these students were not the highest performing, but for some reason, in this teacher's class, they tended to exceed expectations. Why? The second teacher had "teacher pizzazz." Teacher pizazz is the "sauce" of teaching. It's how you empower and motivate students to move mountains, and it leads to high student achievement.

I will preface with this: all of the tools I have provided in this book are fantastic, but they will not work without teacher pizzazz. This will NOT be in your teaching manual or education program, but it is in the Rookie's Playbook, and I want you to find your own teacher pizzazz. This ties strongly to authenticity, being yourself, but also creating buy-in for students. Why should they buy your product? If you aren't excited about the content, why should students be? I'm not saying that you have to be this super excited person, but you need to find a way to get students excited about what you have to offer and bring that heat daily.

As a teacher, you are an actor, salesman, and content specialist all in one, because students will only perform to the bar that we set. Create conditions where students want to go hard for you and buy your product. As a coach, I would often hear from educators that kids "just aren't motivated" and "don't want to do the work," but I know that every student can be reached with the right formula. Every student has the capacity and desire inside of them. As educators, it is our responsibility to figure out how to access that capacity and desire.

As humans, students, you and I alike operate on the same radio station. WIIFM. What station is that, you ask? What's In It For Me FM! Most of us are willing to go the distance if we find a benefit for us in it. One of the mistakes I made early on was I tried to get students motivated by what mattered to me, which was a strong education. Some students bought in to that idea, but a lot of students didn't. I had to learn about what they valued. As previously stated, creating buy-in has a lot to do with knowing your audience and what matters to them. I quickly realized that some students might not have been excited about math, but they were excited about more zeros being added on in their bank account (i.e., money!). I used what they valued to get them motivated about math.

Consider yourself a salesman, and your goal is to sell your product and convince your customers (i.e., your students) to buy the content you are selling. Here are some key components that are essential to being a great salesman of your product:

1. **Be knowledgeable and excited about your product.** It is imperative that you deeply understand your content. It builds credibility with your audience and the buyer. According to Business Queensland, knowing your product is one of the most essential

sales tools. You want to paint the picture of someone who is an expert in their content. Just like we want our students to be learners, we have to take on a similar mindset and continue to build our knowledge of the content. Another benefit of being an expert is it builds trust with your customers and with students. Think about the importance of when you buy a certain product—say, for instance, Chick-fil-A. They are the experts on chicken, so we trust them and are more willing to buy their products.

2. **Know your audience and students.** This is essential to selling anything. This piece really centers around building strong relationships and understanding where your student is coming from and what matters to them. This requires some work in getting to know them. This was a game changer in terms of moving the data in my classroom because it helped me figure out what was the most essential thing for them. Just like with sales, the customer tells you what angle to go in terms of conversation. This is the part that often gets missed. I definitely missed the mark,

because I thought that knowing my product was more than enough to get the job done.

3. **What's the button that will create the buy-in?** After you know your audience, you want to identify the button that will create the buy-in for your students. One of the best coaches I had—Coach Lowery—had figured this out masterfully. He had unique relationships with each one of us and knew what it would take to move us to the next level. He would give some players an earful, while others, he would take on the role of teacher and guide them to the proper place because he knew they were sensitive. Considering the success of that season, he had figured out the button to push in each one us to get us to achieve at a high level and actually want to do the work. It's not about treating kids the exact same way, but more about providing them with what they need to reach their peak performance.

Insight into my button: On the first day of school, I would write four numbers on the board like such:

7.50 per hour @ 40 hours per week	$75,000	$750,000	$7,500,000

I would ask: "How much would each person make a week?"

Students would start feverishly calculating.
75000/52(weeks) = $1,442
7.50 x 40 = $300 per week, 750,0000/52 weeks = 14,423, 7,500,000 = 144, 233

Next, I would ask the students: "Why are they paying this person $75,000 versus $7.50, or even $7.5 million or $750K?"

Students would give all kinds of answers, and what I would be looking for is this person with more zeros solves complex problems and has to be a critical thinker. If they didn't say that, then I would say it. I would then proceed to say, "What am I saying to you all? I'm not saying there is anything wrong with an hourly job or salary. To make the big bucks, you need the skill of critical thinking and the ability to solve **complex problems.** That's why people pay the big bucks—for people to solve a very specific problem. With that being said, this year, I'm going to teach you how to be a critical thinker and solve complex problems. Can I help you do that this year? I have something that you need." It was game on!

This was my bread and butter, and very rarely did I have problems with students not being willing to go the distance in my class. Because of my ability to create buy-in, I produced some amazing results each year—even from students that were projected to perform poorly. The key was the teacher pizazz and convincing students that not only did they need this material, but they had the capacity to do it.

Practice: Determine the answers to the guiding questions:

- What's my content, and what more do I need to learn about it in order to become an expert?

- What do I need to learn about my students in order to identify what they need?
- What is the button I need to push within my students to move the needle toward academic achievement?
- What are my students' top three values? What's at the top of the chart? How can I incorporate that into my lesson?

GAME TIP #29: BOTTOM BUN OF THE SANDWICH: CLOSE YOUR LESSON WITH A BANG!

About eight months ago, I started working with a business and communication coach named Mel B. Cook. During that time, I was in the Toastmasters International Speech Contest. I sent her videos of me speaking, and her feedback changed the game. I had a powerful message, and I had the audience engaged. However, I forgot about the closing. She challenged me to sum up my three key messages and either provide a call to action, quotes, or a story to drive home that key takeaway. She explained that the audience remembers what you say last, so it's important to close with a strong ending. I took her feedback, and I won the contest and moved on to the next round of the competition. It was the closing that elevated my speech to another level because I stamped the key points and left the audience with something to remember. When you consider your lesson, you want to do the same with your class.

Every day, you want to have some form of a strong closing. It's an opportunity to cement the learning, and it allows students to connect the dots of the day's learning experience. Even if I did not get through my intended lesson plan, I would adjust and close based on what content we worked through. Another benefit of closure is it allows you to assess whether the students "got it."

I want you to take a second and think about your favorite movie and the scenes that really stick out to you. What was the big idea of that scene that you thought about? I imagine it vividly sticks out in your mind. Similarly, you want to think about the big idea that you want students to walk away with as a result of experiencing your lesson. What do you want students to know, understand, and do differently from your lesson? Use this as an opportunity to gather evidence and determine any misconceptions that students may have from the lesson. You definitely don't want to leave the students hanging. Too often, teachers focus so much on the implementation and other components of the lesson that they forget about the closing.

There are several tools you can utilize to close the lesson. Here are a few suggestions from my class:

- **Exit Ticket:** Create a task that gives students an opportunity to apply what they learned from the lesson. I usually did not grade these for accuracy. Instead, I was looking for who was close to the objective, who was a little off the road, and who was in a different vehicle. I used these to gather evidence and adjust my lesson for the next day's class.

- **Classroom Discussion:** Create an opportunity to hear student voice and summarize the key ideas of the lesson.

- **Error Analysis:** Give students a problem that is completely wrong with potential misconceptions. Then have the students give an argument for why the answer is incorrect and explain the correct way of approaching the problem. If they can analyze and explain their solution method, then they know the content. Visit mentalfitzness.com/resources for some tools and additional strategies on how to close a lesson.

Practice: Return to your objective of the lesson. Identify the closing activity that will get you toward that intended outcome. Complete the task and identify what mastery will look like for this activity.

PART VI

STAT SHEET STUFFERS

"STAT-SHEET STUFFERS AREN'T ALWAYS SUPERSTARS. COME TO THINK OF IT, A LOT OF THEM DON'T COME CLOSE TO QUALIFYING FOR THAT LABEL. THE ONES WHO REMAIN ARE ATHLETES BUILT ON PRODUCTION AND PRODUCTION ONLY."

—GIANCARLO FERRARI-KING

STAT SHEET STUFFER

ONE OF THE THINGS you'll discover early on in your teaching career is that sometimes you have to learn the hard way by making mistakes. But there are some things that, if you know them ahead of time, you'll save yourself some stress and heartache. I want to share some of those stories and tools, even though they are not necessarily in your teacher education program. These are what I call "stat sheet stuffers," and they're used to help you improve your game. According to Bleacher Report, *"stat-sheet stuffers aren't always superstars. Come to think of it, a lot of them don't come close to qualifying for that label. The ones who remain are athletes built on production and production only."*

I'm not asking you to be a superstar this year—you are already on your way to becoming a Prime Time Player (PTPer). However, I want to provide you with practical tools to help you thrive in year one. These will likely not be in your teacher education program, but they are essential tools you can use to help you become an effective teacher.

GAME TIP #30: CLAPBACK GAME

Kids are much more aware than we are as adults. This is one of the many reasons why I love working with students. They often don't have the filters that we have as adults in terms of what's appropriate to say. For example, we may see someone's outfit that we don't like, but more than likely, we are not going to burst out and scream to that person, "Hey, I hate your outfit!" However, my students would sometimes say what their honest thoughts were, which I invited them to do. Honestly, I wanted my students to bring their full, authentic selves to my class.

Understand that with their honesty, students may also try to push your boundaries. Think about when you were a student. You learned which teachers commanded respect and who you could probably run over if you wanted to by how they responded to your attempt to get off track. The same applies to your classroom.

The clapback is not so much about being the Wicked Witch of the West as it is about gaining respect. According to Merriam-Webster, the definition of a clapback is "*a quick, sharp, and effective response to criticism.*" In other words, the goal of the clapback is to *Shut. It. Down.*

You heard it—"shut it down!" The key to the clapback is having a quick, witty response to not only set a boundary, but to let them know you will not be distracted by their attempt to get the lesson off track. Just be prepared, because kids are going to try you. But it's all about your response and how you handle it. You want to have some back pocket clapbacks for when certain situations happen in class. I also used them to motivate my students to get going and become engaged. Now, I will preface this by saying that different grade levels require different clapbacks. I was a high school teacher, so mine were adjusted to my audience. You want to consider the same for your specific grade.

Here are some examples of clapbacks that I have used:

Statement or scenario	Clapback
Is today a free day?	"Of course, it's free! I'm not charging you anything for this great teaching and learning."
After returning from a break	"This is not 'new year, new me.' This is new year, same me, and you know you don't talk when I'm talking."
You do too much!	"You don't do enough."
That's not fair	"A fair has rides and games, honey. This is life."

GAME TIP #31: LESS IS MORE: DO NOT YELL AT THE KIDS

One time I was observing a teacher and a student had a cell phone. The teacher noticed and walked over to the student's desk. The student was refusing to hand over the phone, so the teacher started to get loud. The student said some "words" and refused to give the cell phone up for at least 2–3 minutes. As I watched, my patience began to wear thin because I wanted to "shut it down." After the class, the teacher and I talked. The feedback I gave him: do not yell, and do not go back and forth in an argument with a student in front of the whole group.

My first year, I would often try to get students to respect me by yelling. Hear me loud and clear: do not yell. It does not work, nor does it build respect with your students. They are not going to be any more inclined to listen to you if you're yelling. Think about when you are communicating with someone. Are you more likely to listen to someone who is screaming at the top of their lungs, or someone with a cool, calm assertiveness? Keep the same thing in mind when you think about communicating with your students. Just like you want respect, provide that same respect to your audience. When we yell, we don't offer mutual respect. I have seen the screaming matches in the middle of class go completely left. I have seen it become a shouting match between the adult and student, and before you know it, the student says something that is embarrassing to the teacher. By this point, the classroom is completely off track, and no teaching or learning is taking place.

Accept the notion that "less is more." The more you scream, the more you lose control and leverage over your classroom. One good tip to help keep the yelling at bay is to know yourself and your triggers. It requires a ton of self-management to be a teacher because your buttons will be pushed. Being self-aware will help you navigate and manage yourself effectively; that way, you don't lose your temper and the respect of your students.

The second tip is I would encourage you to not engage in terms of arguing with a student. Have a contingency plan or policy to address said behavior. Set your boundaries, and keep it moving. Let's go back to the cell phone example. By having a policy in place and a contingency plan, you potentially eliminate some of those issues. If I had a student who produced a cell phone and refused to give it up, I would tell them to either hand over the phone and I would return it by the end of the class, or I would give a referral to the administration to handle the phone. This also sets the example that you mean business.

GAME TIP #32: TAKE A TOUR OF YOUR STUDENT'S NEIGHBORHOOD

I have been in relationship school for the past four months, and it has been a life changer. One of the tools we've learned to utilize is how to LUFU: **L**isten **U**ntil the other person **F**eels **U**nderstood. An important step in using this tool is "getting the other person's world" and really understanding "what's up" for them. Learning about another person's world is going to be imperative as a teacher. This was one of the breakdowns in my opportunities for success in year one. I thought I could just teach my students without taking the time to understand who they were and where they came from.

I assumed that students should think like me, act like me, talk like me, and it was a major failure on my part. I spoke earlier about how I assumed that students should "do math like me," as if I was the goddess of math. I made assumptions about their ability because they used calculators, and my teacher did not allow us to use them. One of the key pillars of communication is knowing who you are speaking with, understanding another person's worldview, and speaking in a language that works for them.

I suggest taking a tour through your student's neighborhood so you can get more context on what their daily life is like. This will provide you an opportunity to better understand their world and invites empathy and compassion. One of the most valuable lessons I learned from teaching is compassion. It taught me how to care for someone outside of myself. Because I understood what some of my students were up against, it created a keen sense of awareness that sometimes I was one of the few people in their lives who was being an encouraging voice, so I knew I had a big responsibility.

According to Edutopia, *"To show compassion to students is to take the time and effort to understand their perspective, while continuing to make choices that are best for their learning experience."* Having said that, you don't want to be so sympathetic that you lower your expectations. I've seen cases where the bar is lowered because a teacher may feel sorry for students. I used some of their challenges and experiences as fuel to inspire and motivate them. It is my belief that teaching is just not teaching, but it's a tool to learn to think critically and create opportunities for yourself. You want to value and understand their unique perspectives and life experiences. I never told my students that their ideas were wrong, so to speak, but I would often use the analogy that if you can convince me the sky is green with evidence, I'm okay with it. Basically, the point here is to take the space to learn about your audience. I was familiar with the surrounding areas my students came from because I grew up in the same region. (I taught at the same high school I attended.) It really created a connection and understanding between us. After all, we are who we are because of our unique environments and life experiences.

GAME TIP #33: SELF-CARE 101

As a teacher, you are a master manager. We complete grades, we manage students, we wear many hats, and, at times, it can feel extremely overwhelming. Submit this form, turn this in, complete grades. I'm not going to lie, it felt like a lot for me.

My first year, I found myself taking home a boatload of homework to grade each night. I'd stay up late and try to prepare for the next day. I felt like I was going crazy trying to handle it all. Teaching is a noble profession, and we have literally selected a career in which we take care of the hearts and minds of children, which requires a LOT! Please don't forget that. And, in the midst of all of the responsibilities we have to manage, you want to ensure that you are taking care of your most valuable asset—YOU!

You are in a field where we are trained to give our heart and soul each day, which makes it that much more essential to take care of yourself. Here are a few tips to help with self-care:

- **Own that you are your most valuable asset!** As the saying goes, you need to put on your own oxygen mask before helping others put theirs on. That same rule applies to teaching. I recently read an article that stated before a school holiday or break, teachers tend to be more on edge and have less patience, which speaks to the emotional effort required to teach. Please take care of you!

- **Identify what your needs are in terms of filling up your cup!** This is imperative because everyone's needs are different. For some, taking a walk, meditating, listening to music, or picking up a hobby can help them feel rejuvenated. It's important to know yourself and what things are needed to help you feel full and restored.

- **Get a mentor.** Keep in mind that it's great to have someone in your corner as a thought partner who can provide positive support and tips to help you make it through challenging moments. This journey is not meant to be done alone. Please seek out help!

- **Schedule the time to take care of yourself.** I find when things are on my calendar, they actually happen. Take the time to schedule your cup-filled activities on your calendar and DO THEM!

- **Leave work at WORK.** The work isn't going anywhere, so leave it at the office. You need time to relax and rest just as much as you need to work and complete your many tasks.

GAME TIP #34: FIND A "STUDENT PLUG"

When I used to travel, my dad had a client that worked in the hotel industry. He had done such a great job as her attorney that it left an impression on this woman. She said that anytime he or any one of us needed a hotel, we could get a friends and family discount. It was awesome! Once, I went to Atlanta, stayed in an amazing hotel, and enjoyed that hotel for a cost-efficient rate. Similarly, I have another friend, Stephanie, whom I call whenever I want to know about the best restaurants in town or a cool spot for a "date night." These two people are each what I call a "plug," because they plug you into—or hook you up with—the information for that specific area.

As a teacher, you want to find a "student plug." They are the students who give you insight into valuable information that you may not have access to normally. For example, one time, my brother Phillip—who is a teacher as well—had given an exam, and one student got a 100 on the exam even though he was failing most of the year. My brother suspected that maybe the student had cheated. Phillip couldn't prove it at first, but two periods later, his student plug came into his classroom and told him that two students in that class had cheated on the exam. He now had proof from his inside source, and he was able to address the situation. He would not have known that without his student plug.

Referring back to my infamous cell phone story about the student who prank called me from inside the classroom, I couldn't figure out why the other students were laughing. My student plug let me know after class that I had called the wrong number and wasn't speaking to a parent. No way would I have figured that out on my own. I thought the students were laughing because they were just being silly, as most ninth graders are, but my plug gave me insight into what had actually happened. Often, this person will emerge out of the blue, so you may not even have to go looking for them. They will give you more insight and intel into the world of students, which will help you immensely in the classroom.

GAME TIP #35: YOU WILL MESS UP, AND THAT'S OKAY!

This year, right now, I need you to give yourself permission to mess up. It will happen. The unique thing about teaching is a lot of the things you learn as a teacher will be from the mistakes that you make, so please be kind to yourself. If you are reading this book, I'm assuming that you have been pretty successful up to this point in your life. Maybe you made good grades, was a successful athlete or dancer. Similarly, I had been pretty successful prior to teaching as an athlete, former NBA manager, and student. Conversely, in teaching, I was on the struggle bus pretty often, but it helped me transform as an educator. It's common for new teachers to struggle because of the challenges they are presented with each day. It may be the first time in your life when you put in max effort and *still* mess up, AND IT'S OKAY.

This is one of the key pieces that make teaching very different from other professions. In basketball, I could spend hours in the gym and see results almost immediately. Teaching, not so much. My first year, I had this seventh-period class where I struggled with classroom management. I took the position in the middle of the year, which created its own set of challenges. I started off the class being way *too flexible*. I had expectations but would negotiate with students on them. Students would ask for the hall pass, and I gave it to them without thought. I had no structure and paid a hefty price for it. Within the first thirty days, I was stressed out because I couldn't seem to get a hold of classroom management, and it wasn't just this particular class that I was struggling with, it was multiple classes. Imagine my stress level, screaming at the top of my lungs each day and leaving with a headache. I was trying everything in the book to get my students under control, yet I still could not figure it out. I tried assigned seats—it didn't work. I tried screaming—it didn't work. I felt like a complete failure and asked myself, "Why can't I figure this teaching thing out?" The truth is I failed, but I wasn't a failure. In order to be successful in anything, failure and losses are a part of becoming a great teacher. No one told me that, but I'm telling you so that you can prepare for that challenge and normalize your mistakes.

In our society, we often make mistakes the "wrong" way, but it's my belief that problems are a privilege. We need to experience obstacles in order to grow and transform ourselves into the best versions of ourselves—both professionally and personally. I can guarantee you that without those sore throats and being hoarse, I would not have learned to manage my classroom efficiently.

In summary, it's not a matter of if you mess up, but when. And it's okay. Grace and compassion for yourself are needed during that first year because the mistakes are coming. Even the most successful educator was, at some point, a rookie and made plenty of mistakes. You are no different. There are no perfect teachers around here, and the L's are what will make you the phenomenal educator that you are striving to become.

GAME TIP #36: FILE 13—WHAT'S YOUR GRADING PLAN?

During my first year, I spent most of my time grading papers. Each day I would take home a backpack full of them. One day, I was having lunch with two of my colleagues, and there I sat again, grading more papers. My colleague, who shall remain nameless, said, "Are you grading *everything*?" I told him, "Yes, I try to," and he introduced me to File 13. He said, "You simply cannot grade everything— some things go to File 13. I thought, *File 13? What the hell is that?* He then told me that File 13 was the trash can, and, sadly, I had to dump some of the work in File 13.

Totally not one of my brightest moments, throwing students' work away; however, I learned that it's beneficial to have a plan for how you will grade things. Some things I graded for accuracy, others I simply checked for participation, and so on. You have to figure out what works for you. My grading plan became this: The "Do Now" quiz was graded for mastery, so I graded it as is. For the exit ticket—or closing activity—students received a participation grade, which means if they did it, they got full credit. However, to guide tomorrow's lesson, I was determining what misconceptions surfaced and checked for mastery by looking at their responses.

Classwork was a participation grade and another opportunity to check if the kids were "in the car" and provide real-time feedback to my students.

Notice I did not grade every single paper. I had specific assignments that truly mattered to guide students in moving toward our targets and goals. To save yourself time and energy, you want to identify what assignments matter in terms of grading. You do not have to grade everything. Below is a framework to help you think about your grading plan. Remember, if you know the purpose of why you are utilizing each assignment, it is easier to grade and be more strategic in how you move. As you can see in the plan below, I was looking for student mastery in every assignment. The key was how I graded it. Same with you. How will you grade each assignment?

Assignment Type	Student (How it will be graded)	Teacher Purpose (Grade expectation)
Do Now	Graded	Assess mastery and readdress misconceptions from yesterday's

		lesson, cumulative content mastery
Classwork	Participation	Assess mastery, surface misconceptions, and provide real-time feedback
Homework	Participation	Address misconceptions, random grading on one problem
Exit Ticket	Participation	Assess mastery and gather data for tomorrow's lesson
Quiz and Test	Graded	Assess cumulative or summative mastery, surface misconceptions, and potential corrective instruction plan

GAME TIP #37: UNDERSTAND THE ROLES OF TEACHING: YOU ARE NOT JUST A TEACHER

Teaching is not the only role that you will hold as a teacher. We wear many hats in this profession. I literally thought that I would just teach math each day, and that is not the case. You do a lot more than teach a lesson. We are engaging and interacting with human beings who have developing brains, which invites emotions and other things as well.

I often tell people that to be a teacher, you have to become a master manager. Coming in with the idea that I would only teach was extremely overwhelming because I didn't understand all of the many moving parts in the role. You will have the roles and responsibilities that come with teaching, such as lesson planning, grading papers, and the like. However, the roles that I'm speaking of are the additional roles that may not necessarily be in your teacher preparation manual.

- **Salesperson:** It's important to sell your content to students and get them to buy in and be engaged. As teachers, it is our responsibility to figure out how to get the students interested in doing the work. I have heard educators say, "I can't get my students to do it." Well, I would like to challenge you to start off with the perspective of: "I can and must identify a way to motivate them. If one way doesn't work, I will try another." As a teacher, there is a huge responsibility in the sense that we cannot allow the challenges and obstacles that may arise to stop us from achieving our objectives.

- **Surrogate parent:** At times, you may have to stand in as a surrogate parent. Sometimes, my students did not have a parental figure in their lives, so you may have to be that support for them. In one of my classes, I noticed that one of my student's pants were extremely short, so I stepped in and gave him several pairs of pants.

- **Role model:** You are an example of excellence. I held this role near and dear to my heart because I knew that some students did not have that person in their life—someone being a positive influence. This is my tagline as an educator: "I Build Efficacy." Self-efficacy is the belief that I can produce a desired result. I BELIEVED until they did.

- **Motivational speaker and influencer:** As a teacher, you are in front of students each day. As you think about selling your product, (i.e., your content), you want to bring your full self with charisma and teacher pizzazz. You will need to bring some personality to this work. No one wants to learn from the boring teacher standing at the board—sorry. Bring your own personal passion to this work. If you aren't passionate or excited, why would your students be?

- **Coach:** A coach's job is to disrupt the pattern. You will need to be relentless in your expectations, hold students to a standard of excellence, and push them to the potential that they may not see in themselves. My motto is: "I know your secret," which means I know how strong your mind is and how capable you are, and I will not let you off the hook.

- **Private Investigator:** I promise you I can spot a cell phone being used in my classroom from a mile away. I am not the most detailed person—on the DISC assessment, I only have 10 percent of it in me. However, as a teacher, I am so aware of the details. This is a skill set you'll want and need to have to constantly have a pulse on your classroom.

GAME TIP #38: WHEN YOU HAVE A MELTDOWN, DO THIS....

If you are reading this section, I imagine you've had a meltdown. You may be wondering, *Did I make the right choice by becoming a teacher? Is teaching really this hard? Maybe I should enter another profession. Will I come back next year? Am I cut out for this?*

And, to answer your last question, yes! You are cut out for this. Here is a key point to remember: every seasoned teacher, administrator, superintendent—even your principal—has, at some point, been a first-year teacher, and they survived. You will too. I'm not going to lie, the first year can be tough, and just like any challenge, it invites a wide range of emotions, hence the title of this section.

Trust me when I tell you, they will be coming. The key is how to navigate them in a healthy and resilient way. You have more bounceback than you know. And remember, as stated in the section, some of the mistakes we make as teachers are essential to helping us grow as professionals.

First, give yourself permission to be messy. Another lesson I'm continually reminded of in relationship school is that when you are learning something and working with humans, it's going to be a messy process. You will fall down, go a little bit further, become stagnant, cry, laugh, get back up again, and that's okay. You are learning new information. Just like when a baby falls down, they don't stop walking. They get up and try again. However, learning to walk is a messy process, and you are a baby teacher learning to teach. Often, new teachers expect to be amazing immediately and don't understand that being messy is a part of the journey, so they leave the profession. If you can make it through the messiness, you will be a great teacher.

Breathe and feel your feelings: Deep breathing helps reduce fatigue and anxiety and provides better stress management. Just about every relaxation, calming, and meditation technique utilizes deep breathing because it physiologically calms our nervous system. Take a deep breath and be present with what you feel. It's a great way to slow yourself down and feel your feelings, rather than ignoring them.

Ask for help: There are several people that can help you this year. As we discussed earlier, a mentor or coach is essential to have on your team. According to ASCD, teachers need professional *and* emotional support. Please ask for help. A good mentor can give you the space to share your feelings and/or frustrations and possibly provide you with practical tools to address the problems.

Connect with other first-year teachers: I promise that you are not the only one facing challenges as a first-year teacher. Utilize your network of new teachers as a resource to share your experiences and support each other. You may feel less alone knowing that you are not the only one, but also get some insight into some success stories.

GAME TIP #39: MY CLASSROOM IS OFF THE CHAIN: TIME TO RESET

When I was younger, I loved to play on the Nintendo Entertainment System. There were only two buttons on the system. Power, to turn it on, and Reset, to start the game from the beginning. I would be working through and playing the game, and one of my siblings would hit the reset button. I would be so angry because I would have to start the game completely over. You may have a moment this year when you need to push the reset button.

Maybe you are saying to yourself, "I started the year off strong. I thought I had it going and then it all started falling apart." Your classroom is what I call "off the chain"—or, in layman's terms, "out of control." You can get back to teaching, I promise. It's not easy; however, it can be done. I had a similar experience and thought I'd never recover, but I want to let you know how I bounced back.

I spoke to my mentor because I had two classes that were cutting up, and my classroom management skills were so wack that the students rarely listened to anything I had to say. I wanted help, and I wanted it desperately. She recommended that I have a talk with the class and start grading EVERYTHING to send a clear message that I meant business about working hard in class. It was a headache at first because I didn't really have the time. However, after a long chat with my students and grading every single assignment, my classroom management slowly started to shift for the better. Why did it work? I pressed the reset button. You may be thinking, *How? How do I press the reset button?*

You'll want to start with an honest assessment of where you are. Then, depending on where you stand, you may want to seek out feedback from your mentors or teachers who have strong pedagogical knowledge. This way, they can provide you with practical advice to manage your challenges.

Here are a few strategies you can use to reset:

- **Entry Routine:** Students would normally just walk into my classroom from their other classes. However, at one point, my students were coming into class and taking an extra long time to get into their task for the day. It seemed they'd rather spend most of their time talking to other students. After 2–3 days of that, I knew it was time to press the reset button. For the first few days, to emphasize the key idea of structure in entering the classroom, I shut my door. Therefore, students had to line up on the locker until the bell rang. The students couldn't stand it because it forced them to line up on their lockers like eighth graders—versus merely walking in and getting on task.

- **Off-task behavior:** Give students new assigned seats and have a clear flow of the lesson. Maybe even switch up the flow to reengage them with the content. When you have a clear flow, there's less of an opportunity for students to get off task and start doing other things.

- **Speech! Speech!:** A little motivation never hurt anybody. My intro speech to this is: "We have had fun this year, *and* we are going to make some key adjustments to get us back on track." The key here is communication—you want to highlight a compelling message to inspire them to do the work to elevate.

These certainly are not the only ways to reset your classroom, so feel free to utilize what works for you. I would recommend working with a mentor or coach on this specific task of pressing the reset button.

GAME TIP #40: RESET 2.0: IT'S A BREAK OR HOLIDAY, ALLOW ME TO RE-INTRODUCE MYSELF!

Allow me to re-introduce myself! My first few years as a teacher, I would come back after the break and dive right into the content. I thought we could pick up where we left off. It did not go well, my friends. It was almost as if my students had completely forgotten how to operate in the classroom. This type of reset is a little different than the previous one. This reset is simply to reassert yourself and your expectations after a long break. This is similar to day one.

I would also recommend taking some time to reflect prior to the return date. Identify what's working and where are some opportunities to grow in your classroom. Do you need to tighten up your entry routine? Did you notice one part of your classroom management procedures that you need to change? If so, now is the time to do it.

What I began to realize was, before you jump into work, take the first half of day one to do the following to help with re-asserting yourself and your expectations.

- **Check in with students and ask how their break went.** This is a great opportunity to build relationships and show that you care. As I reflect on my own teaching experience, I can't help but feel like this was a missed opportunity on my part. If students have something exciting to share—or even something challenging—this is important information for you to know, considering that relationships are the lynchpin to great teaching and learning.

- **Revisit goals, purposes, and targets for this school year.** I would often use this as an opportunity to give my students an opening day speech 2.0. I would remind them of what we were shooting for this semester and explain how certain components would change in class. For example, I knew that during the second semester, I was going to raise the bar even higher because assessments were around the corner, and I wanted to make sure my students were ready. I would also remind them of my expectations and let them know that I believe in them and their abilities.

- **Re-establish and reinforce classroom management, systems, and procedures.** Schedule some time to review your classroom rules and procedures with your students. Just like on the first day of school, you want to stick to your policies and procedures to provide structure so you can teach your content. Sometimes students forget over the break how everything flows in your class, and this is a great way to remind them.

Agenda Item	Plan
What's your plan to check in with your students? Refer to mentalfitzness.com/resources for suggestions.	

What are the goals for today's first day back? What are the targets for the school year that you want to remind your students of? What are the key points you need to emphasize and re-emphasize to your students?	
When and how will you revisit your classroom management policies and procedures? Are there any adjustments before the break that you need to re-emphasize?	

GAME TIP #41: PROFESSIONAL LEARNING: COMMIT TO BECOMING A PTPER

After mastering the first three years of teaching, I was consistently a level five teacher, which means that students had more than above average growth in my class. Because I was one of the top teachers at my school, our professional learning community coaches asked if they could record my class and norm on ratings with the district rubric. Knowing that my scores would be pretty good, I gladly said yes. For most of my observations, I was consistently in the top tier. Well, the group rated my video, and my scores were not great. Where I normally would score a five, I scored mostly threes. It was an eye-opener for me. Here I thought I was this great teacher with very few flaws, but I actually had areas in which I needed to improve. I took the feedback from my colleagues and adjusted my instruction. It made all the difference in my practice. Not only did my observation scores improve, but my data was off the charts that year. How did that happen? It's because I was willing to accept constructive feedback and learn something new.

One of the ways to level up your practice and learn something new is to participate in professional learning or development courses. Let me preface this by saying that you want to ensure that it's effective, solid professional learning. However, it's my belief that you can learn from anyone and any session.

Several months ago, I participated in an interview panel. We saw at least ten candidates. Upon first glance, there were several resumes where I thought to myself, *Wow, this is a strong candidate, and it's going to be a tight race to picking the right fit for the position.* Each interviewee came into the room, and there was one question that tripped up some of the candidates, creating a clear separation between those who were good and those who were outstanding. The question was: "Tell me about a professional learning session that you attended, and how did you apply what you learned to your current role?"

It was amazing to listen to some of the responses. It was also evident when someone had invested in their own professional growth. The race was getting close, and the lead was between two candidates. Then the last candidate arrived, and she smashed the competition. She responded to every question with precision, presence, and personality. One thing was evident, though. She knew her content deeply and was well equipped for the job. After discussing each candidate, it was clear who the top choice was for the position—the last candidate.

After we had finished our selection, I asked the panel how she was so well equipped for the interview, even though her resume did not necessarily show the skill set that she clearly had. The answer: she had attended every single professional learning session that had been offered throughout the year. She was committed to her development as a professional, which enabled her to smash the competition and separate herself from the pack.

How does this apply to you? Commit to growing yourself as a professional and attend sessions to help you become a better teacher. In the book *The First Days of School*, the authors explain that teachers who commit to developing themselves as PTPer teachers earn 35 percent more than teachers who don't. That's crazy! We may believe we have all the answers however, there's always room for growth. Once we feel like we have all the answers, we can't grow anymore. We all need a little help. I certainly do. Even now, in my current role as a coach/consultant, I am constantly seeking out professional learning sessions to develop myself as a mathlete. Find a great professional learning session and attend it. It's a phenomenal way to learn something new and grow as a teacher.

GAME TIP #42: ESTABLISH YOUR OFF-SEASON PLAN

When I was in fifth grade, I told myself that I wanted to play Division I college basketball. However, by the time the summer of my junior year rolled around, I had no offers on the table. Each year prior, I would take the summer off and just relax and not work on my game, and it cost me. I decided that summer that I was going all in on improving myself as a basketball player so I could earn a scholarship to college. I would wake up each morning at 5:00 a.m. to run, lift weights, do push-ups, and play basketball outside of practice. By the end of my senior season, I had three offers to play collegiate basketball. How did I go from zero offers to three? The off-season plan. I was committed to growing and elevating my skill set, and I saw the impact of that work. You want to do the same thing as a teacher each off-season. Below is a thinking map to help you identify your off-season plan:

1. **What's on your scouting report?** Assess yourself honestly. You may also want to seek out a coach or mentor to provide feedback.

What did I do well this past school year? Where am I doing well so far this year?	Where do I need to improve? Where have I had a hard time?

My BIG GOAL for the next school year is (e.g., use a planner, learn my time tables, etc.):

2. **What's your "why"?**

I want to accomplish my BIG GOAL because…

3. **Create a plan.** Identify what you need to do in order to grow in these areas. Do you need to attend a professional development

session, up your training, or work with a
coach? Be specific.

This summer, I commit to the following to
<u>LEVEL UP</u> my teaching game (e.g., doing fluency
activities, attending tutoring, etc.):

1. _____
   _____
2. _____
   _____
3. _____
   _____

---

4. **Have a GROWTH MINDSET & GET
   TO WORK! (Work your plan.)**

*"A **growth mindset** is the belief that intelligence
improves through study and practice."*
—Carissa Romero

Success can only happen with the proper mindset
to support it.

GAME TIP #43: CALL ALL OF YOUR STUDENTS' PARENTS DURING THE FIRST WEEK OF SCHOOL

I was attending a faculty meeting during the first week of school, and the principal was giving us tips to help us be successful for the school year. One of the things he recommended was calling all of your students' parents or guardians the first week. Well, folks, I was so afraid of having another year like year one that I was crazy enough to do it.

I called each parent and shared my name, my expectations, my teaching style, my goals, and how excited I was to teach their child this school year. I explained to them that if they needed anything at all throughout the year, they could reach out at any time. It was a game changer.

I already had an ally with the parent prior to the hustle and bustle into the school year. The parents knew my name, and I created a positive relationship so that if anything would come up as we progressed throughout the year, I had already laid the foundation of "my intentions are to help your kiddo win," which will go a long way. You are going to stand out with the parents, too. This is because when teachers call a parent, it's usually for something negative rather than positive.

I'm sure you are thinking, *When will I have time to do this? Wow, this seems like a lot.* It's more on the front end versus the back end. These phone calls are going to make your job so much easier as it gets challenging throughout the year. For example, the following Monday after I called all those parents, several of my students said, "You called my mom or dad this weekend!" This displayed several things that would help me in the future. One: It shows the students that you will call their parents if necessary. Two: You said positive things about them to their parents, which is always a win. And three: You have won over a parent or guardian who will likely support you if anything comes up. I want to challenge you to find time to make the calls. Each call did not take more than 3–5 minutes, so just do it!

Practice: Create a script for your introductory phone calls and make the calls! Below is a sample prompt that you can use for your phone calls.

Hello, may I speak to Ms. Or Mr. _____. My name is _____ and I am so excited to teach_____ your subject this year. I just wanted to briefly touch base with you so that you can know who I am and what to expect from me. I'd like to share a few goals. Is now a good time?

- Expectations (homework, be on time, put forth best effort)
- Teaching style (I'm somewhat like a coach, I believe in building students' confidence through math, so I am relentless in my expectations)
- Goals (growth in math, state exam, or any other vital information)

Closure: Thanks again for taking the time to chat with me. I'm looking forward to working with _____. I would love your support and helping her/him succeed this school year. If you need anything throughout the year, please feel free to reach out to me. Are there any last questions you have for me before we hang up?

"FEEDBACK IS THE BREAKFAST OF CHAMPIONS!"

—MONICA JORDAN

GAME TIP #44: BE COACHABLE AND OPEN TO FEEDBACK

IN HIGH SCHOOL, I was one of the top players on my basketball team. However, when I arrived at college, that was no longer the case. I received feedback quite often when I was a high school player, but when I got to college, I received feedback ten times as much. Everything became extremely technical and detailed. It was quite a challenge for me. However, what I began to learn was that players who were coachable, who were able to implement the feedback and learn the system, received the most playing time. I adjusted and learned the importance of feedback and coachability immediately, because I wanted to be on the court.

This will be a critical component for you as a rookie teacher. You do not know everything. Be willing to learn from those who have already been in the game for a while. One unique aspect of teaching is we often steal ideas from one another. I have learned some of the most amazing concepts by watching other teachers. Having a coach or another teacher that you can collaborate with is so important as you begin this journey, but it's also imperative to be receptive to the feedback you receive. Feedback is the breakfast champions, and most of the people who have great success are willing to receive feedback and continue to evolve and grow themselves. I have seen new teachers who were resistant to receiving feedback and were not coachable. Most of the time, those teachers continually struggled, because they weren't willing to receive help and lacked an open mind. One of the best ways to improve in anything is by receiving high quality feedback and implementing it.

This tip is about having a growth mindset and openness to receiving feedback to help you improve as an educator. You do not have to do this alone! If you can't find someone to help you, reach out to me—I got you. Here are a few ways to shift your thinking about feedback and coachability:

1. Feedback allows you to level up. We often have blind spots that we are unaware of, and a great coach or mentor can help you identify

some of those things and provide tips to address some of those blind spots.

2. Receiving feedback does not mean something is wrong with you or that you are a failure. It is simply an opportunity to improve your practice and possibly see things differently. I would often get defensive in my personal life when I received feedback because I wanted to be perfect and thought, *Well, if I'm not perfect, then there must be something wrong with me.* That's just not true. As an athlete, I received feedback, and because of my continuous implementation, I was able to earn a full athletic scholarship to college and all-conference honors. That would not have happened without feedback.

3. Be a learner. As previously discussed, you are going to make a lot of mistakes, and that's okay. However, the key is to be open to learning from those mistakes. This may be the first time that you go all in on something and the results don't come immediately. I had to be willing to use my mistakes as an opportunity to grow as an educator. This is a practice I do with most areas in my life. As a new teacher, I was a sponge to everything

that I received. I would try out different strategies to determine what worked for me.

4. Coachability saves you a **MASSIVE AMOUNT OF TIME**. During my first year, my students often did not "get" the lesson by the end of the class, and I continued to wonder why. My mentor observed me, and she gave me some feedback that was centered around my checks for understanding. After, she allowed me to watch her implement the strategy, and it was a game changer. I saw my student data slowly but surely rise. I had been struggling with students not understanding the content for most of the year, but with her quick, targeted feedback, I was able to make those adjustments immediately. Now, I want to add that the feedback doesn't always work immediately. Sometimes, it takes a little longer because you are making it work for you, so be patient with yourself.

GAME TIP #45: REMEMBER, YOU ARE BUILT FOR THIS

We finally made it to the end! Remember, when it comes to teaching, you are the X factor. The plans or coaching won't work without you, and I want to tell you that "YOU GOT THIS!" It's going to be hard. You will have meltdowns and doubt your own ability, but you will make it.

I was speaking to a new teacher recently, and he said, "This is by far the hardest thing I've done, and I really want to get this right. If I can do this, I know I can do anything." I respected his willingness to own that teaching is hard shit. And I want to remind you that if you picked up this book, I know your secret. I know your potential, your desire to figure it out, and your willingness to learn how to thrive as a teacher.

I want you to know that teaching comes with a huge responsibility, and we have a huge task in front of us. I want to challenge you to find a way to keep going. What's going to help you succeed is your willingness to continue to find solutions when you hit a roadblock. I've seen teachers that blame the students or other factors for their lack of success, but, ultimately, it's our responsibility to find a way to get the job done. You can and you will! If Edison would have quit on the light bulb, we would be walking in the dark. He said, "*I have not failed 10,000 times. I have not failed once. I have succeeded in proving that those 10,000 **ways** will not work. When I have eliminated the **ways** that will not work, I will find the **way** that will* *work.*" I challenge you to find a way, grasshopper. You are built for this!

You were the brave one who decided to jump into the arena and try to navigate this terrain of changing the lives of human beings that could possibly shape our futures. I want to applaud you for your willingness to get in there, and I want to remind you that this process of learning can be messy. It's not a linear, one-hit-and-quit fix. It requires some failures, some wins, and, sometimes, some bruised egos to learn this teaching game. However, you can handle it. When it gets tough—and it will—sit down and remind yourself that you are built for this shit. Then, watch yourself go from a rookie to a seasoned pro in no time!

ACKNOWLEDGMENTS

To you, the reader, thanks for reading this book! Thank you to everyone who has supported me on this journey. To all of my mentors: Ms. Holmes, Ms. Dickenson, and Ms. Reid. You set the bar for excellent teaching and supported me along the way. To every basketball coach and teammate that has taught me about life through sports. Without its many life lessons, I would be a fraction of who I have become. To my parents, thank you for showing me that anything is possible with discipline and hard work. You were truly trailblazers in your families and set the bar high for me. To Jen and Phill, thanks for being the best siblings in the world and always being a soundboard for my eccentric ideas. To Erin Abraham and Julie Ebling, who took the time to experience my book and provide high-quality suggestions to make this project great. To my coach, Mel B. Cook, who continually challenges and held me accountable every step of the way. Last but certainly not least, to my favorite human being Christina, thanks for always having my back and supporting me, and seeing things in me that I had yet to discover. I love you for many lifetimes and beyond.

ABOUT THE AUTHOR

Andrea "Fitz" Fitzgerald is an educator, consultant, author, and coach known for moving educational data and building the self-efficacy of individuals. With over a decade of experience, she truly believes that, to improve results, one must build the whole teacher by enhancing their self-awareness and efficacy with intentional challenge and support. As a teacher, Fitz was one of the key contributors to Kirby High School, being selected as a Gold Gain and Silver Gain School for three consecutive years, as well as State of Tennessee Reward School. As a result of her contributions, she earned the Effective Practice and Incentive Spotlight Teacher. She continues to demonstrate a proven record of moving student data from the lowest percentile to proficient by building strong relationships and self-efficacy of students and educators. Fitz currently resides in Memphis, Tennessee. She enjoys running, reading, and spending time with her doggies. To connect with Fitz, visit:

- Website: mentalfitzness.com
- Instagram: @mentalfitzness
- Facebook: @mentalfitzness

THE
ROOKIE'S
PLAYBOOK